Italian Lakes

by Richard Sale

Richard Sale took up writing full time after
spending many years as a research scientist.
He has contributed to a number of
magazines, chiefly on outdoor topics, and of
the 35 or so books he has published, most
are travel guides to European destinations,
including titles on the Italian Lakes and
Milan. Richard lives on the Cotswold Way
in Gloucestershire.

Above: *The harbour at Tarbole, Lake Garda*

AA Publishing

Above: Italian ice-cream tastes superb, whether sold at a modern 'parlour' or from an old-fashioned bicycle

Written by Richard Sale

First published 2001
Reprinted Aug 2001, Aug 2002
Reprinted Jan 2004. Information verified and updated. Reprinted May, Aug and Dec 2004.

© Automobile Association Developments Limited 2004

Published by AA Publishing, a trading name of Automobile Association Developments Limited, whose registered office is Southwood East, Apollo Rise, Farnborough, Hampshire GU14 OJW. Registered number 1878835.

A02483
Atlas section and cover maps
© Mairs Geographischer Verlag/Falk Verlag, 73751 Ostfildern

Colour separation: Chroma Graphics (Overseas) Pte Ltd, Singapore
Printed and bound in Italy by Printer Trento S.r.l.

Find out more about AA Publishing and the wide range of travel publications and services the AA provides by visiting our website at www.theAA.com/bookshop

Contents

About this Book

KEY TO SYMBOLS

✚ map reference to the maps found in the What to See section

✉ address or location

☎ telephone number

🕐 opening times

🍴 restaurant or café on premises or near by

Ⓜ nearest underground train station

🚌 nearest bus/tram route

🚆 nearest overground train station

⛴ ferry crossings and boat excursions

✈ travel by air

ℹ tourist information

♿ facilities for visitors with disabilities

💷 admission charge

↔ other places of interest near by

❓ other practical information

➤ indicates the page where you will find a fuller description

This book is divided into five sections to cover the most important aspects of your visit to Italian Lakes.

Viewing Italian Lakes pages 5–14
An introduction to Italian Lakes by the author.
Italian Lakes's Features
Essence of Italian Lakes
The Shaping of Italian Lakes
Peace and Quiet
Italian Lakes's Famous

Top Ten pages 15–26
The author's choice of the Top Ten places to see in Italian Lakes, each with practical information.

What to See pages 27–92
The five main areas of Italian Lakes, each with its own brief introduction and an alphabetical listing of the main attractions.
Practical information
Snippets of 'Did you know...' information
3 suggested walks
2 features

Where To... pages 93–116
Detailed listings of the best places to eat, stay, shop, take the children and be entertained.

Practical Matters pages 117–24
A highly visual section containing essential travel information.

Maps
All map references are to the individual maps found in the What to See section of this guide.
For example, Stresa has the reference
✚ 36A4 – indicating the page on which the map is located and the grid square in which the town is to be found. A list of the maps that have been used in this travel guide can be found in the index.

Prices
Where appropriate, an indication of the cost of an establishment is given by £ signs:
£££ denotes higher prices, **££** denotes average prices, while **£** denotes lower charges.

Star Ratings
Most of the places described in this book have been given a separate rating:
000   Do not miss
00   Highly recommended
0   Worth seeing

Viewing the
Italian
Lakes

Above: *Steamers are an attractive
way of seeing the lakes*
Right: *In the early morning, scanning the
sports pages is essential*

Richard Sale's Italian Lakes

Above: *The lakes are ideal for watersports*

Alternative Names
The lakes have alternative names, derived from those given them by the Romans, which the visitor will occasionally see. Maggiore is Verbano, Como is Lario and Garda, Benaco. The Roman names for the two smaller lakes, Orta and Iseo, were Lacus Cusius and Lacus Sebinus respectively.

Great Violin Makers
Although the lakes area has its own musical heritage, the lover of the violin will want to visit Cremona, just 40km south of Brescia, where Stradivarius and other great violin makers worked.

The Italian Lakes are superbly sited for the traveller; just a short distance from the high peaks that mark the border between Italy and Switzerland – take the cable car from Maggiore's shore and Monte Rosa, the second highest mountain of the Alps, seems close enough to touch; an equally short journey from the great Renaissance cities of the Lombardy Plain – Cremona and Mantua; and within reach of Venice. From Lakes Maggiore and Como it is just an hour or so southwards to the treasures of Milan; from southern Lake Garda it takes even less time to reach Romeo and Juliet's Verona. Between the two are Brescia, with some of the best Roman remains in Italy, and Bergamo, an almost complete, virtually traffic-free, walled Renaissance town. North of Lake Garda lie the spiky towers of the Brenta Dolomites.

Focusing on these nearby places, however, may lead one to ignore the lakes themselves. The enviable climate (warm summers and crisp winters) and natural beauty of the area have attracted visitors for centuries. Rich and artistic Romans built villas here, a tradition which was revived in the 19th century – a string of villas, from the sumptuous to the simple, being built along the shores. The combination of water, sunshine and the fertile soil at the lakeland edge allowed the villa builders to cultivate magnificent gardens. Some of these are now internationally renowned and attract visitors from all over the world.

Yet despite these advantages shared amongst the lakes, they are all quite different in character. Orta, hemmed in by high ridges, is secretive; Maggiore busy, yet peaceful. Lugano is very Swiss, Como very beautiful and elegant. The eastern lakes, Iseo and Garda, are the holiday lakes, Garda especially – the beaches of its eastern shore are beloved of sun-worshippers. Add food at its Italian best, the highly drinkable wines from Garda's shore and lake steamers that take the strain out of local excursions, whether you explore or choose a more relaxing visit, the Italian Lakes offer the perfect holiday destination.

Features of the Italian Lakes

Lake Maggiore

- Despite the name, Maggiore is not the biggest of the lakes (that's Garda) – but it is the longest.
- From Magadino, in Switzerland, to Sesto Calende is 65km.
- The lake covers 215sq. km.
- At its deepest point the lake is 372m deep.
- About 15 per cent of the lake lies across the border in Switzerland.

Lake Lugano

- The lake is 36km long, but very narrow, rarely more than 2km wide.
- The maximum depth of the lake is 288m.
- The causeway which carries the road and railway across the lake cuts it into two separate areas.
- About 60 per cent of the lake lies in Switzerland.

Lake Como

- At 410m, Lake Como is the deepest of the lakes.
- The deepest point, which lies off the shore of Argegno, is 300m below sea level.
- The lake has an area of 148sq. km.
- Because of its shape, the lake's shore line measures 170km, the same as that of Lake Maggiore.
- Although the lake has two arms, only one of them – the Lecco arm – has an outflowing river.

Lake Garda

- Lake Garda is the largest lake, covering 370sq. km.
- The lake has a maximum depth of 346m.
- Despite its size, the lake's shoreline measures only 125kms.
- Garda is the only lake without a significant island, though it does have a handful of tiny islets.

- The River Po, into which all the outflowing rivers from the lakes empty, is Italy's longest river at 420km.

- With a population of about 1.3 million, Milan is Italy's second biggest city after Rome.

Above: *From Orta San Giulio it is a short boat ride to Lake Orta's famous island, Isola San Giulio*

Economic Factors

Milan is the economic capital of Italy. Though it is most famous as a business centre and for its fashion houses, the city also has many heavy industries. Como is the centre of Italian silk production. The mulberry bushes which feed the silk 'worms' grow in the Brianza, the triangle of land between the two arms of Lake Como. Brescia is a centre for steel and engineering companies, as Bergamo is for textile manufacturing. But despite these industries, the major activity of the lakes area is tourism.

Sport and Leisure

- Anything to do with water
- Cycling
- Walking
- Climbing
- Skiing in winter

Essence of the Italian Lakes

Visitors to Lake Garda soon become familiar with the fishtail battlements of its castles

The Italian Lakes lie close to the great medieval trade route across the Lombardy Plain, and the region saw its share of the feuds and intrigues which characterise that period of history. Como fought a long war with Milan, and Milan fought Venice on the waters of Lake Garda. Before that the Romans and the barbarian hordes who defeated them had come this way. After the flowering of the Renaissance, with Italy carved up between rival kingdoms, great battles of the Risorgimento (Unification) were fought here. Later conflicts, social and artistic movements also touched the area. But though the tides of history have occasionally left their mark, these have merely added a historical dimension to what is, scenically, one of the most beautiful areas in Europe.

THE 10 ESSENTIALS

If you only have a short time to visit the Italian Lakes, or would like to get a really complete picture of the country, here are the essentials:

The Italian climate is perfect for alfresco dining

• **Take a boat ride.** With all that water it would be a crime not to, but there are other advantages – some lakeside villas and villages look best from the water.

• **Go uphill to view the lake.** Lake views from the shores are splendid, but to see the lakes at their best it is necessary to climb to one of the retaining ridges.

• **Go shopping.** It may sound like a cliché, but for leather Italy has few equals and for silk Como is the place. And then there are the fashion houses of Milan....

• **Eat alfresco** – with the climate and Italian cooking how could anyone not?

• **Buy an ice-cream.** All towns and most villages have shops selling ice-creams and sorbets in the wonderful flavours of local sun-ripened fruits.

• **Go for a walk.** Not only do the high ridges above the lakes offer superb views of them, they are a paradise for the flower lover.

• **Learn to windsurf.** The lakes have some of the most dependable winds in Europe. The air is warm even if the water is cool, and there is no chance of being blown miles out to sea.

• **Visit a villa or garden.** One of the great features of the lakes are their villas and gardens, and no visit would be complete without visiting at least one.

• **Take a stroll.** Italians share with the Spanish the habit of an evening stroll – to meet friends or just to be seen.

• **Visit a town.** There is a temptation while on holiday to avoid the hustle and bustle of a town. Italian towns are different, however, being virtual open-air museums. The lakes cannot boast the great Renaissance towns of Tuscany, but Bergamo, Verona and central Milan are very fine places.

Milan's vast, ornate Duomo (cathedral) was described as an 'imitation hedgehog' by writer D H Lawrence

The Shaping of the Italian Lakes

c9000 BC
The last Ice Age completes the work of shaping the land begun by earlier ones. Rivers that had flowed south to the plain of the River Po, cutting valleys through the Alpine foothills, are replaced by glaciers. These deepen the valleys massively, but also deposit ground-up rock – moraine – at their edges and snouts. When the ice finally retreats, the edge (lateral) moraine forms fertile shores to the lakes formed behind the dams of terminal moraine.

6000 BC
The area is inhabited by Neolithic (New Stone Age) peoples, who leave carvings on the rocks of the Val Camonica near Lake Iseo.

Pliny the Younger, famous for his letters and his long speeches

4000 BC
Early Bronze Age people settle in the area. One group, settling around Brescia, has been named the Remedello culture (after the first identified site) because of their distinctive burial goods.

2000 BC
Later Bronze Age peoples have also been named from particular sites near the lakes: the Golasecca culture from southern Lake Maggiore and the Comacine from Lake Como.

1000 BC
The lakes area is settled by Celts and Etruscans.

390 BC
After the founding of Rome (legend dates this to 753 BC) the Romans expand northwards, but in the 4th century BC the Gauls cross the Alps. They sack Rome in 390 BC and create Cisalpine Gaul, which includes much of the lakes area.

300 BC
The Romans defeat the Gauls, bringing northern Italy into the empire. The remains at Brescia (Roman Brixia) date from the 1st century AD.

c84 BC
The lyrical poet Catullus is born at Verona and builds a villa at Sirmione.

AD 23
Pliny the Elder is born at Como. His nephew (Pliny the Younger, born in 62) probably had a villa on Lake Como.

313
The Edict of Milan grants religious freedom to Christians. In 391 Theodosius makes Christianity the official religion of the Empire.

5th century
After Theodosius splits the empire into two halves, the western empire falls to the 'barbarians' of the north. These include the Longobards or Lombards, who settle in what is now Lombardy. Legend has it that the Lombards arrived after being sent a crate of local wine and details of the area's defences by an aggrieved eunuch at the emperor's court in Constantinople.

8th century
Charlemagne defeats the Lombards and founds a Frankish kingdom in northern Italy.

9th century
Carolingian (the line of Charlemagne) rule ends. The Lombards retake Lombardy, but are subsequently defeated by the Magyars (from Hungary).

951
Otto I, King of Saxony, invades and takes control of northern Italy.

12th–15th centuries
Era of the city states. The Viscontis and Sforzas rule Milan, while the della Scala (Scaligeri) control Verona and Lake Garda. Milan defeats Como in the Ten Years War (1118-1127). In the early 15th century Milan and Venice fight a 30-year war.

1527
François I of France takes control of northwest Italy, but Hapsburg Charles V defeats him in battle and sacks Rome. For 150 years Milan and the western lakes are controlled by the Spanish, the eastern lakes by the Venetians.

1701–13
The War of the Spanish Succession results in the Savoy controlling north-western Italy, with Austria taking Lake Garda.

French troops cross into Italy during the Risorgimento

1796
Napoleon frees northern Italy of Austrian rule, but it is restored after his defeat.

1842
The newspaper *Il Risorgimento* (The Awakening) is first published in Turin leading to a groundswell of popular desire for the unification of Italy.

1859
In battles near Solferino, a French-Piedmontese army defeats the Austrians. In a smaller battle near Como an army under Garibaldi defeats another Austrian force.

1870
Italy is unified under King Vittorio Emanuele II.

1919
Treaty of St Germain

after World War I gives Austrian Trentino to Italy.

1936
'Pact of Steel' is signed between Mussolini and Hitler.

1943
After taking Italy into war against the allied forces Mussolini falls from power. Although Germany installs him as head of a 'republic' centred on Salò on Lake Garda's western shore, the new Italian government declares war on Germany.

1945
Mussolini attempts to escape Italy by road along Lake Como's western shore, but is arrested at Dongo and summarily executed.

1946
King Vittorio Emanuele III abdicates. Italy becomes a republic.

1957
Treaty of Rome creates the Common Market. Milan emerges as the economic centre of the new Italy.

1990s
The Northern League (Lega Nord) gains support for its proposal to split the wealthier northern states off from the rest of Italy.

11

Peace & Quiet

Monte Baldo

Monte Baldo, on Lake Garda's eastern shore, is occasionally known as the 'Botanical Garden of Italy' because of the variety and profusion of species which grow on its flanks. Two parks, the Lastoni Selva Pezzi and the Gardesana Orientale, have been set up to protect the plant life. The former is at the base of the ridge, the latter higher up, the plant species changing as altitude increases. In the lower park there are olive groves, then holm oak and Mediterranean pine, while higher up there exists a rich collection of alpine flower species. Monte Baldo boasts three species which are unique to the high ridge – the *Anemone baldensis*, the bedstraw *Galium baldensis* and the speedwell *Veronica bonorata*.

Gazing across Lake Garda towards Monte Baldo

For many visitors the gardens of the great villas that are dotted along the shores of the lakes offer the peace and quiet they seek. But those looking for a more natural landscape must move away from the water's edge, climbing to the open hillside of the ridges which define the lake valleys or visiting the local natural parks.

The High Ridges

In the high valleys of the Val Grande Natural Park, in the pre-Alpine mountains that define Lake Maggiore's western edge between Pallanza and Switzerland, and in the high reaches of Val Brembana and Val Seriana the walker will hear the whistle of marmots and may see chamois. There are golden eagles and alpine choughs here, black grouse and rock partridge, snowfinches and alpine accentors and, in the Bergamo valleys, little bustards. The flora is true alpine, with mountain poppies and buttercups, pale pasque flowers and rare species of daisy and saxifrage.

Easier to reach are the hills of the Grigna and the Resegone which stand above Lake Como's eastern shore. These mountains are of dolomite, a magnesium-rich limestone that forms a thin soil that supports a distinctive plant life. Most visitors will want to find edelweiss, but the real enthusiast will be looking for more exotic flowers. These include several varieties of gentian, Rainier's bellflower (*Campanula raineri*), which is restricted to the

Grigna and the Bergamesque Alps, the rich scarlet mountain gladiolus (*Gladiolus sylvestris*), pink cinquefoil (*Potentilla nitida*) with its delicate five-petalled flowers, burning bush (*Dictamnus albus*) with orchid-like flowers, and the aptly named devil's claw (*Physoplexis comosa*). There are also several unusual species of saxifrage. Birdwatchers will be a little disappointed as there are few unusual species here, most sightings being of alpine choughs and black kites, though the latter are just as likely to be seen over the lake itself. Be cautious if you think you have seen chamois here – they are much more likely to be feral goats.

The animal lover is less well served as the lower slopes of the valleys are built up or farmed, while the upper slopes have a limited range of alpine species. Between the two are the mountain forests, chiefly beech, arolla pine and larch. Here finches thrive, together with black woodpeckers, Tengmalm's owls and the rare wryneck. There are wild boar and red deer here, and the lucky visitor may see the elusive beech marten. Equally elusive, but still seen occasionally, is the fire salamander.

The ridges above the lakes are superb for walking. This is the Resegone above Lecco

The Lakes

The lakes themselves are home to several species of duck, including great-crested grebes and red-breasted mergansers – visitors are actually discouraged from feeding the mallards, which are increasing in number to epidemic proportions. There are flocks of black-headed gulls, kingfishers work the inflowing streams and wallcreepers can occasionally be seen at the lake edge. The lake margin is also a good place to look for swallowtail butterflies. The lakes are also home to more than 20 species of fish.

Marshland

Birdwatchers will be more interested in visiting the Pian de Spagna, the marshland area at the head of Lake Como. The Spluga Pass, to the north, is used by migrating birds as a way across the Alps, the Pian being a noted spot for the birds to rest before continuing south. Species likely to be seen outside the migration periods include mute swans (this is Italy's only breeding site), bittern, purple and grey herons, marsh harriers and eagle owls. Similar species can also be seen in the Brabbia Marsh near Lake Varese (there are great reed warblers here too), the two natural parks on either side of the River Ticino where it leaves Lake Maggiore, and on the Sebino peat bogs at the southern edge of Lake Iseo.

Monk's hood, a typical flower of the high ridges

13

Famous of the Italian Lakes

Bergamo's most famous son, Gaetano Donizetti

Gaetano Donizetti

Gaetano Donizetti was born in Borgo Canale in Bergamo's Città Alta in November 1797, the fifth child of six in a poor family with no musical tradition. He joined a charitable school at which choirboys were trained in Bergamo Cathedral when he was nine, and was immediately recognised as musically gifted. At the age of 18 he was sent to study music at Bologna, returning to Bergamo when he was 20. His first opera was performed in Rome when he was 25 and he was soon being commissioned to write works for opera houses all over Italy. For twenty years Donizetti was the leading Italian composer, his reign ending with the performance of Verdi's Nabucco in 1842. By then Donizetti's health was already failing. He returned to his Bergamo home and remained there for the rest of his life, dying in April 1848. He was buried in the local cemetery, but his remains were moved to the church of Santa Maria Maggiore where a fine memorial had been erected to him. Donizetti's most famous works are *Lucia di Lammermoor* and the comic opera *L'Elisir d'Amore*.

Alessandro Manzoni

Alessandro Manzoni was born on his father's estate close to Lake Como in 1785. He was sent to boarding school when he was five and it is said that his mother never visited him, deserting the family when Alessandro was seven to live with another man in Paris. Though it is claimed that this was a defining moment in the young boy's life, he did join his mother in Paris when he was 20, living in the city for many years. Manzoni had begun writing poetry by the age of 16 and was writing in earnest during his stay in Paris. He married in 1808 and two years later moved back to Italy, living in Milan. Though he continued to write, his most famous work, *I Promessi Sposi* (The Betrothed), was not published until 1827. It was an instant hit, both in Italy and throughout Europe. Sir Walter Scott claimed it was the finest book ever written and it is now considered to be the greatest Italian novel of the 19th century. Though Manzoni edited the book several times, he did not write anything else of any significance. Troubled by increasingly poor health, by the death of his beloved first wife and seven or their nine children, and by the death of his second wife, he lived unhappily in Milan until his death in 1873. He was given a state funeral and Verdi wrote his Requiem to commemorate the first anniversary of his death.

Catullus

Catullus, the greatest of Rome's lyrical poets, was born in Verona in about 84 BC and had a villa at Sirmione. Catullus is credited by some experts with the invention of the love poem, his works being dedicated to 'Lesbia', a married woman with whom he had an unsatisfactory love affair. He is said to have died of a broken heart at the age of 30 when Lesbia finally rejected him.

The Plinys, Elder and Younger

Pliny the Elder was born at Como in AD 23. He was a Roman statesman and scholar most notable for his *Natural History*, an encyclopaedia of the natural world. Pliny was killed while observing the eruption of Vesuvius in AD 79 which destroyed Pompeii. Pliny the Younger (AD 62–113) was the Elder's nephew. He was a senator and is famed for his writings on the Roman state. Ironically he also wrote a description of the eruption which killed his uncle.

Top Ten

Above: *The church
of Santa Caterina
del Sasso on
Lake Maggiore
is one of the
highlights of
the area*
Right:
*Enjoying a
lakeside stroll*

1

Bellagio

Bellagio is best seen from the lake

The poet Shelley claimed the 'Pearl of the Lake' was the loveliest town not only on Lake Como but in the world and many since have agreed.

✠ 36C4

✉ The point where Lake Como splits into two

🍴 Bilacus, 32 Via Serbelloni (££) ☎ 031 950480

🚌 Buses from Como

🚢 Regular lake boats

♿ Fine on lake front, but no concessions in steep section of village

Villa Melzi

🕐 Gardens and chapel only Apr–Oct daily 9–6:30

✋ Moderate

♿ Few

Villa Serbelloni

🕐 Gardens Apr–Oct daily. Guided tours only, at 11 and 4

✋ Moderate

♿ Good

A narrow road runs along the eastern shore of the Como arm of Lake Como, offering a drive which is at best tiring, at worst positively hair-raising. By the time Bellagio is reached the visitor may be too exhausted to notice. The town also presents its poorest aspect to those who approach by road. But the approach by water...

Bellagio sits at the very tip of the Punto Spartivento, the 'point which divides the wind', strung out along a narrow terrace on the western side. As a result, when it is approached by boat, the whole village is laid out for the visitor's inspection. The lake front is an array of beautiful buildings, red-roofed and with pastel-shaded walls, above which rises the campanile of the 11th-century church of San Giacomo. At one end of the village is **Villa Melzi**, the finest neo-classical villa on any of the lakes. At the other end, **Villa Serbelloni**, now owned by the Rockefeller Foundation, is equally impressive. Legend has it that the villa stands on the site of one of the two which Pliny the Younger had on the lake.

The villas may be the architectural highlights of the village, but there is much more. Though now possessing a plethora of souvenir shops – many selling locally made silk – and occasionally overcrowded because of its popularity, there is still a real Bellagio beyond the lakefront tourist traps. A small maze of steep, sometimes cobbled streets awaits to delight and confuse the visitor. Wander at leisure enjoying both the old-world charm and the occasional stunning views of the lake.

2
Duomo, Milan

Dominating the centre of Milan, and with a forest of statues, the Duomo (Cathedral) is one of the wonders of northern Italy.

On 17 September 1387 a group of Milanese armourers gathered in what is now Piazza Duomo to begin work on the building of a new cathedral for the city. The armourers were followed by the city's drapers, bootmakers, butchers and others as each craft lent its voluntary efforts to the new building. The Duomo was built of marble from the Candoglia quarry (near Gravellona Toce, close to Lake Maggiore's western shore), the blocks of stone being marked AUF before being shipped by lake, river and canal to the city. The letters stood for *ad usum fabricae* – for building use – as the stone was exempt from local taxes, but so thinned out was the building work that *auf* became a local term for a long wait or for working for nothing. In fact, it was 400 years before the building was completed.

The Duomo Milan is 157m long and 92m wide, the third largest in the world – after St Peter's and Seville Cathedral – and has over 3,000 statues and spires, a veritable forest of stone. At the highest point is the Madonnina, a gilded copper statue of the Madonna. So revered is the statue that by city regulation no building is allowed to rise above it. The Madonnina stands 108m above the square and can be viewed at close quarters by those who follow the 919 steps to the roof (there is a lift for those who find the prospect daunting). The view from the roof of the spires and the city is superb.

Inside the cathedral, a red light high in the nave marks the position of a True Nail from Christ's cross. It is brought to ground level every year so that it may be viewed. The brass strip set in the cathedral floor is illuminated by the sun shining through a hole in the roof at noon on 21 June and 21 December. In the crypt lies the body of San Carlo Borromeo, one time archbishop of Milan whose colossal statue can be seen at Arona (▶ 43).

✝ 31D2

✉ Piazza Duomo, Milan

☎ 02 86463456

🕓 Mon–Fri 7–7, Sun 1:30–4:30

🍴 Al Mercante, Piazza Mercanti 17 (££) ☎ 02 8052198

🚋 1, 2

♿ Few

✋ Free; Crypt and Treasury cheap

A visit to the roof of the Duomo allows a close-up view of the Madonnina

3
Isola Bella

Isola Bella has a variety of curious statues

Some are appalled by the 'wedding cake' of Isola Bella, but many more marvel at the sheer audacity of its creation. Few can stay neutral.

In 1620 the closest to the shore of the three islets off Stresa on Lake Maggiore was rocky and occupied by only a few fisherman and their families. There were two small churches, but it was a hard life for the islanders as there was almost no soil for growing food. At that time, one of the Borromean counts, who owned the islands and much of the nearby mainland, decided to transform the fishing island into a pleasure garden. He died in 1638, but his vision of creating something worthwhile from the barren rocks was taken up by his brother, Count Carlo III. Carlo had boatloads of soil transported to the island, his architect using it to create a ten-terraced island designed to look, from the shore, like a great ship sailing down the lake. The Count named the island for his wife, Isabella, but the unwieldy Isola Isabella was soon dropped in favour of today's version, which also has the advantage of translating as 'beautiful island'.

On the island the Count and his sons – the entire endeavour took decades; indeed work was not finally completed until 1958 – built a vast baroque palazzo, its numerous rooms hung with art treasures. Some of these rooms are exquisite, some exquisitely awful. The Napoleon Room (where he and Josephine slept in August 1797) and the Luca Giordano Room are peaceful and understated; the Great Hall with its Wedgewood blue walls is superb; the Tapestry Gallery with its 16th century Flemish tapestries is extraordinary. But the Music Room is wildly overdone and the grottoes beneath the palace, decorated with shells and curious stucco, is alarming (though the collections here are fascinating). Outside, the gardens are a treasure of overstatement. The statuary of the terraces is appalling, the whole organised in taste so bad it becomes appealing. But the gardens themselves are very good and the views wonderful.

✝ 36A4

✉ Offshore from Stresa on Lake Maggiore

☎ 0323 30556

🕐 Easter–Oct daily 9–12, 1:30–5:30

🍴 Elvezia (££) ☎ 0323 30043

🚢 Regular lake boats from Stresa, boat 'taxis' also available.

♿ Few

✋ Expensive

4
Orta San Giulio

Set at the bottom of a steep hill and with a marvellous view across Lake Orta, this little village is one of the prettiest on the lakes.

In the 4th century two brothers, Giulio and Giuliani, arrived at Gozzano, near Lake Orta, to spread the gospel. Giulio continued to the lake, drawn by the story of evil dragons that lived on an island at its centre. He amazed the locals by spreading his cloak on the water and then stepping on to it, using it as a raft. Giulio drove the dragons away and stayed on the island, setting up a hermit's cell and preaching to the lake fishermen (▶ 40).

The village from which the saint set out is now known as Orta San Giulio. It is a traffic-free, charming place with steep streets and picturesque houses, some with external frescoes. One such is the Casa Morgarani, the House of Dwarves, the origin of its name lost in time. The main square, Piazza Motta, is set at the lakeside. It is cool and tree-shaded, and from it boats can be hired for the short trip across to the saint's island. There are good restaurants and cafés here too.

The village's artistic treasure lies away from the lake, set on the hill above the houses. On the Sacre Monte a woodland path threads a way past 21 chapels which contain almost 400 life-size terracotta statues illustrating scenes in the life of St Francis of Assisi. Work on the chapels and statues began in the 17th century, but the Sacre Monte was not finally completed until early in the 19th century.

✚ 36A3

✉ Towards the southern end of Lake Orta's eastern shore

🍴 Sacro Monte, Via Sacro Monte 5 (££)
☎ 0322 90220

🚌 There are buses along the eastern shore which link with southern Lake Maggiore and Gravellona Toce

⛴ By lake boat from Omegna

♿ Few

🖐 Free

From Orta San Giulio there is a marvellous view of Orta's island and the hills of the far shore

5
Piazza Vecchia, Bergamo

37?D3

Bergamo's Upper Town

Colleoni e Dell'Angelo, Piazza Vecchia 7 (£££)
035 232596

Funivia from Viale Vittorio Emanuele II in the lower city

Few

Torre Civica

Closed for restoration; check with the Tourist Office for details

Cheap

Although overshadowed by the reputation of Renaissance Tuscany, Bergamo is one of the finest small medieval towns in the country.

A funivia connects the modern lower city of Bergamo to the Città Alta, the Upper City, the ancient town set on a hill to the north of the new city centre. The ride is a short one, no more than a minute or two; but when the visitor steps out at the top he has travelled backwards in time by several hundred years.

Piazza Vecchia – the Old Square – is the heart of the Upper City. The architects Frank Lloyd Wright and Le Corbusier both claimed that the square was the finest from the Renaissance that Italy had. At its centre is the Contarini Fountain dating from 1780 when it was a gift from Alvese Contarini, the Doge of Venice – his position explaining why the fountain is embellished with Venetian lions. There is another Venetian lion on the Palazzo della Ragione, the magnificent building at the southern (cathedral) end of the square. The palazzo dates from the last years of the 12th century, making it the oldest municipal hall in Italy (though it needed considerable rebuilding after a fire in the 16th century). Access to the palazzo is by way of the elegant external stairway. The lion on the palazzo is a replica, the original having been torn from the building and smashed in 1796 when the townsfolk were fed up with Venetian rule.

In front of the palazzo is a statue of the poet Torquato Tasso. To the right – as the visitor views it – is the **Torre Civica** (or Torre del Comune), the town's campanile, built in the 12th century, with a 15th-century clock. The tower can be climbed for a terrific view of the old town. From the Palazzo della Ragione the visitor should cross the length of the square, marvelling at the cunning way brick has been used to create tile-effect paving, to reach the Palazzo Scamozziano which closes the northern side. This fine building was built in the 16th century in fine Palladian style.

6
Santa Caterina del Sasso

Apparently clinging to a sheer rock face above the waters of Lake Maggiore, the church of Santa Caterina is one of the most picturesque in Italy.

✚ 36A3

✉ Close to the village of Reno on Lake Maggiore's eastern shore

🕐 Mar–Oct daily 8:30–12, 2:30–6; Nov–Feb daily 9–12, 2–5

☎ 0332 647172

🍴 Nothing at the site, but on the road to Laveno, a short distance to the north, is Il Porticciolo-Bellevue (££) ☎ 0332 667257

⛴ Regular lake boats (otherwise a car or tour bus is essential)

♿ Very difficult. Those arriving by boat or road must negotiate steps both up and down

✋ Free

In the 12th century Alberto Besozzi, an unscrupulous local man who was renowned as a smuggler and usurer, was crossing Lake Maggiore alone when a vicious storm blew up, capsizing the boat. Besozzi, flung into the water, was in danger of drowning. In terror he promised God that if his life was spared he would repent and live a blameless life of prayer. Miraculously, a wave threw him high on to a ledge on the sheer cliffs near Reno on the lake's eastern shore. Equally miraculously, he landed uninjured.

Good as his word, Besozzi spent the rest of his life – another 40 years – on the ledge, kept alive by food lowered to him in a basket by people who had heard of the miracle, and water from a spring. At one time, when plague threatened the locals, Besozzi prayed for them and they were all spared. In gratitude the locals built a church on the ledge, naming it for Santa Caterina to whom Besozzi had prayed. When he died Besozzi was buried in the church.

The church can be reached by boat, but those who come by road gain the truest sense of the church's position, clambering down numerous steep steps. The church at the base was damaged by a rockfall in the 17th century, but its miraculous nature was further proved when a huge boulder was stopped from demolishing the hermit's tomb by three small bricks which jammed it into a stable position. Built at the very edge of the ledge, the church is a masterpiece of grace and engineering. Inside there are beautiful medieval frescoes and the remains of Besozzi – now the Blessed Alberto – curiously preserved from decay, a remarkable, if somewhat macabre, sight.

Above: *The beautiful frescoed ceiling is one of Santa Caterina's treasures*

Opposite: *The Contarini Fountain in Bergamo's Piazza Vecchia, with the campanile rising up behind*

7
Sirmione

✚ 37F2

✉ At the southern end of Lake Garda, close to Desenzano

🍴 Risorgimento, Piazza Carducci, 5/6 (££)
☎ 030 916325

🚌 Buses from Desenzano

⛴ Regular lake boats

♿ Few

Grotte di Catullo

☎ 030 916157/9906002

🕐 Mar–Sep Tue–Sun 8:30–7; Oct–Feb Tue–Sun 8:30–4:30

✋ Moderate

Scaligeri Castle

☎ 030 916468

🕐 All year Tue–Sun 9–7 (Oct–Mar 9–4:30)

✋ Moderate

A finger of land so narrow as to seem an unfeasible site for a town and a castle from a Hollywood film set combine to create a fairytale village.

From Lake Garda's southern shore a finger of land pokes north into the lake waters. The finger is 4km long and, at its narrowest, little more than 100m across. At its end is a blob of land – like the dot above an 'i'. On this 70ha blob sits Sirmione. The strategic importance of the isthmus was not lost on those masters of war, the Romans, but the Imperial forces had more than one reason for settling here. Just off-shore, from the lake bed about 20m below the surface, a thermal spring gushes water at 70°C; too good an opportunity for the fastidious Romans to ignore. The ruins of the Roman bath house can still be seen. They are called the **Grotte di Catullo**, named for the great lyrical poet Catullus, who is known to have had a villa here and who mentioned the village in his poetry. The allusion to Catullus may be fanciful but the ruins are worth visiting: a small museum holds local Roman finds. Today the waters of the spring feed a spa that treats muscular ailments and sinus problems.

The isthmus maintained its strategic importance after the Romans had departed, and in the 13th century the Scaligeri, lords of Verona, built a castle. Visitors to Sirmione must leave their cars at the apex of the 'i', and walk across a narrow bridge (all non-essential vehicles are prohibited from crossing so that visitors may explore the tightly packed village streets in comfort) and through a medieval gateway which gives the impression that the **castle** itself is being entered. In fact, it stands to the right, complete with a lake-filled moat and an intricate ring of walls which protected supply ships. The walls and towers are topped by the fish-tail battlements that were the trademark of the Scaligeri and with which visitors to Lake Garda and Verona soon become familiar.

Above: *Embarking for a trip on the lake*
Opposite: *The spectacular castle at Sirmione is one of the best preserved in the area*

8
Tignale/Tremosine

37F3

Tignale and Tremosine lie above Lake Garda's western shore. They are connected to the lakeside road, and to eath other, by narrow roads

Madonna di Montecastello

Tignale, above the western shore of Lake Garda

0365 73019

All year Sun 10–12:30, 5–7

Tavernetta Fucine di Leonesio Francesco, Via Fucine, 11, Vesio (Tremosine) (£)
0365 951151

Infrequent buses from the larger lakeside towns

Few

Vesio, a village high on Tremosine

High above Lake Garda's western shore lie two plateaux which offer incomparable views of the lake and a glimpse of another world.

On Lake Garda's western shore the main road (the Gardesana Occidentale) has been hewn out of the rock, sometimes tunnelling through it, sometimes set on an improbable ledge. Heading northwards with Gargagno at your back and Riva some distance ahead, you will soon reach a left turn onto a narrow, winding road which climbs to Tignale. After crossing the plateau, and the side road to Montecastello, the road descends steeply into the valley of San Michele before rising again to reach Tremosine, crossing this plateau before falling sharply to regain the main road.

The journey is about 30km, despite the twisting road, but it is worth the time and effort. On the Tignale road that rises from the lake there are viewpoints from which to savour the panorama.

The Scaligeri, masters of Verona, built a castle on a rock above the village of Gárdola, but this was destroyed and a church raised after miracles at a nearby chapel. Today, the sanctuary of **Madonna di Montecastello** is famed for the view and for its art treasures.

From Tremosine, pass through Pieve, an attractive village with some of its buildings perched above vast drops. From the village the road descends quite normally at first, but then turns sharply to go under itself and through a narrow, dark chasm, offering an extraordinary drive that is definitely not for the faint-hearted.

9
Verona's Listone

A short distance from the hustle and bustle of Verona's famed tourist attractions is a quieter place where the visitor can briefly relax.

The Listone in Verona is an ideal place for people-watching

The visitors' heart of Verona is centred on the squares of Piazza dei Signori, with its Scaligeri tombs, and the Piazza dell'Erbe with its market stalls. From the latter it is a short step along Via Cappello to the Casa di Giulietta, where Juliet's balcony beckons the sightseers.

South of the crush is Piazza Brà, the largest square in the city and one of the largest in Italy. The name is from the Latin *pratum*, meadow, and there is still an area of green at the square's heart. But it is the elegant curve of buildings along the square's western edge that holds the attention. This is the Listone, the social heart of Verona, a graceful sweep of restaurants and pavement cafes. Sit here for a quiet reappraisal of the hectic scenes in the main visitor area, or just to be entertained by the street theatre artists.

At the far end of the Listone is the **Arena**, Verona's Roman amphitheatre, a vast ellipse built in the 1st century AD. From the cafés there is an excellent view of what the locals call the *ala*, meaning wing, the only section of the original three-tier perimeter wall which survived a destructive earthquake in 1183. The Arena, once the site of gladiatorial contests, is now thankfully a more peaceful place: it is the site of Verona's famous annual opera season. At the other end of the Listone, across Via Alpini, is the city's **Maffei Lapidary Museum**, with one of Europe's best collections of ancient inscribed stones.

✚ 37F2

✉ Piazza Brà, Verona – an easy walk from almost anywhere in Verona

🍴 Cafe Opera, Piazza Brà, 10 ☎ 045 8009903 – for a coffee and snack

♿ No problems on the Listone, but few concessions in the visitor sites

Arena

☎ 045 8002304

🕐 All year Mon 1:30–7:30, Tue–Sun 8:30–7 (9–3:30 during the opera season)

✋ Moderate

Museo Lapidario Maffeiano

☎ 045 590087

🕐 All year Mon 1:30–7:30, Tue–Sun 8:30–2

✋ Cheap

25

10
Villa Carlotta

Villa Carlotta has one of the finest gardens in the region

Villa Carlotta is the most famous of the lakes' villas, and with good reason – it's a beautiful villa, elegantly decorated and with superb gardens.

✚ 36C4

✉ Tremezzo, on the western shore of Lake Como

☎ 0344 40405/41011

🕐 Apr–Sep daily 9–6, Mar–Oct daily 9:30–11:00, 2–4:30

🍴 Tremezzino, Via Regina 40, Bolvedro (££)
☎ 034 440496

🚌 Buses along the shore road from Como

🚢 Regular boat service

♿ Reasonable

✋ Moderate

Many visitors arriving at Villa Carlotta assume that the 'C' above the entrance is the C of Carlotta. It is a fair assumption, but wrong: it stands for Clerici, the family that built the villa in the 18th century. With its window-pierced façade, symmetry and entrance stairways the villa is a masterpiece. The Clerici sold the villa to the Counts Sommariva, and it was during their ownership that most of the art that now graces the villa was collected. Later the villa changed hands again, being sold to a Prussian Princess who gave it to her daughter Charlotte (known as Carlotta) as a wedding present. It was Carlotta who laid out the gardens in 1850s.

Inside the villa the artistic highlight is Antonio Canova's *Cupid and Venus*, a marvellous portrayal of tenderness. The interior is also notable for its decoration, particularly the ceilings (some based on designs from Pompeii) which are masterpieces of the plasterworkers' art.

For many, though, it is the gardens which are the main attraction. Here grow more than 500 species of tree and shrub as well as fern and flower beds. There are about 150 varieties of rhododendron and azalea, many of them in Azalea Avenue or trimmed to create hedges. There are also large collections of camellias and wisterias. In summer, the flowers and shrubs make Carlotta the most colourful place on the lakes, while the citrus trees add a sharp tang to the air.

What to See

Above: *The southern end of Lake Como seen from above Cernobbio*
Right: *Old Bergamo's Contarini Fountain offers an impromptu ride*

Milan

Milan, Italy's second city but its unquestioned economic hub, deserves a book of its own. There is a Roman city, *Mediolanum*, named after its position at the centre of the Lombardy Plain and one whose early Christian monuments rival those of any other town. There is the Milan of the Viscontis and Sforzas, that of the Spanish domination and another from the Austrian era. There are marvellous palazzos from the 18th and 19th centuries and the modern commercial city. There is even the Milan whose football teams are the equal of any in Europe and whose stadium at San Siro is worth visiting just to be amazed at its size and elegance.

Which of these cities should be explored by the visitor on a time budget? Perhaps a little of each, the 'must-see' sights which, hopefully, are covered here. As with all large, commercially active cities, Milan can be all pace and movement. But at its heart, in Piazza Duomo and the nearby squares, the Italians find, as always, time for a coffee and a moment's relaxation away from the hustle. The visitor can too.

'Milan e pocu più'
(Milan and nothing more)

Often said by the Milanese to
reflect their view of their city

———————•———————

28

The green walls of Castello Sforesco

What to See in Milan

BIBLIOTECA AMBROSIANA ⭐⭐

The vast Palazzo dell'Ambrosiana was begun in the early 17th century to house the library of Cardinal Federico Borromeo, a member of the family which owned, among other things, the islands in Lake Maggiore. The building is a little severe, but inside there is an excellent collection of art as well as the library. The collection includes works by Brueghel, Caravaggio and Luini, but is most notable for the portrait of the musician Gaffurio by Leonardo da Vinci.

✚ 30C2
✉ Piazza Pio XI. Near to Piazza Duomo
☎ 02 806921
🕐 Tue–Sun10–5:30
♿ Reasonable
💵 Expensive

CASTELLO SFORESCO ⭐⭐

The first castle on this site was built by the Viscontis from the mid-14th century. This building was partially destroyed by the townsfolk on the downfall of the family, but their joy must have been short-lived as the Sforzas soon rose to power and created an even more domineering structure. The Sforza fortress fell into disrepair but was saved from demolition by enlightened citizens and now houses superb collections of art, weapons and armour, and much more. Of the art, pride of place must go to the awesome *Rondanini Pietà* by Michelangelo, while the collection of weapons is one of the finest in Europe. The castle is also worth visiting just for itself. Look up as you enter the Torre dell'Orologio, the Clock Tower. This superb 70m tower is an exact replica of the 15th-century original destroyed when the gunpowder stored within exploded.

✚ 30B4
✉ Piazza Castello
☎ 02 861125
🕐 Tue–Sun 9–5:30
Ⓜ M1 – Cairoli station
♿ Reasonable
💵 Free

DID YOU KNOW?

Michelangelo's *Rondanini Pietà* is unfinished and it is usually assumed that the great man died before completing it. In fact, towards the end of his life Michelangelo became convinced that a mere man could never hope to capture God in art and abandoned the work.

DUOMO (▶ 18, TOP TEN)

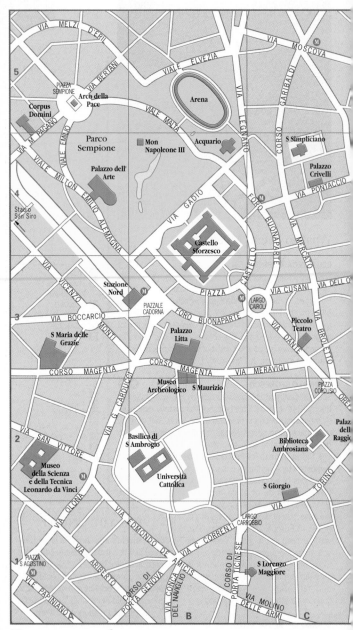

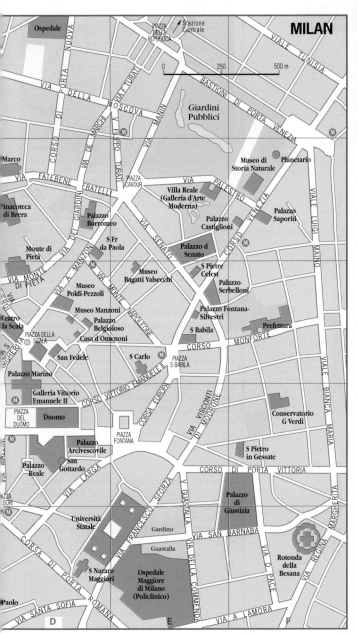

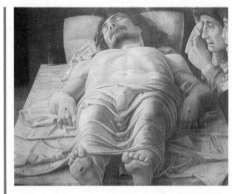

Mantegna's Dead Christ *can be seen in the Pinacoteca di Brera*

🕇 30A2
✉ Via San Vittore 21
☎ 02 485551
🕐 Tue–Sat 9:30–4:50 (5:30 on Sat and Sun)
Ⓜ M2 – S Ambrogio
♿ Few
💷 Expensive

🕇 31D4
✉ 28 Via Brera
☎ 02 89421146
🕐 Tue–Sun 8:30–7
Ⓜ M2 – Lanza
♿ Few
💷 Moderate

🕇 30B2
✉ Piazza Sant'Ambrogio
☎ 02 86450895
🕐 Mon and Wed–Fri 10–12, 3–6, Sat and Sun 3–6
Ⓜ M2 – S Ambrogio
♿ Few
💷 Cheap

MUSEO NAZIONALE DELLA SCIENZA E DELLA TECNICA LEONARDO DA VINCI ✪✪

The museum named after Leonardo houses not only an excellent collection exploring science and engineering but a gallery dealing with his work in aeronautics, engineering and anatomy. The 'conventional' section of the museum includes full-size ships, aeroplanes and trains, and exhibits such as the equipment used by Umberto Nobile on his balloon-borne expedition to the North Pole.

PINACOTECA DI BRERA ✪✪✪

Palazzo di Brera was begun in the early 16th century and is in fine baroque style with a unity that belies the fact that it took over 100 years to complete. In the courtyard is a bronze statue of Napoleon by the artist Canova. This fine work is a prelude to the collection inside which many consider to be one of the best in Italy. Everyone will have a favourite, but by common consent the finest works are the heartbreaking *Dead Christ* by Andreas Mantegna; and the *Madonna with Saints,* which includes the famous portrait of Federico di Montelfeltro (and his equally famous nose) by Piero della Francesca.

SANT'AMBROGIO ✪✪

Legend has it that Ambrogio (St Ambrose) arrived in Milan soon after the city's bishop had died. The contest for a successor was causing feuding and uproar. Ambrogio calmed the crowd, and they were so impressed with his bearing that they decided he should be the new bishop. Ambrogio was not even a Christian at the time, but was hastily baptised and installed as bishop. Soon after, he began work on the church which now bears his name. The present church, a lovely building in Romanesque style, dates from the 11th century although there are sections of much earlier work. Inside, the gold altar by Volvinio, with its relief panels depicting scenes in the life of the saint, is a masterpiece of 9th-century goldsmithing.

SANTA MARIA DELLE GRAZIE ✪✪✪

In 1463 the Dominican Order of friars was given land on which to build a church and monastery. The church, to St Mary of the Favours, is built in dramatic style with a marvellous façade and apse. It has two surviving cloisters, the Cloister of the Dead and the smaller Cloister of the Frogs. The church is well worth visiting, but its famed treasure is within the nondescript building beside it, once the refectory of the monastery. Here in 1495 Leonardo da Vinci began work on his *Last Supper*, which, together with the *Mona Lisa*, have set the seal on his reputation as an artist. Always the innovator, Leonardo chose to paint on to dry plaster rather than using the more common technique of painting quickly on to wet plaster. Though this allowed him more time – it took two years to complete the work – it meant that moisture between the plaster and the paint lifted flakes of paint off the wall. Within 20 years the painting had begun to deteriorate. There have been several attempts at restoration, the last only just completed.

✚ 30A3
✉ Cenacolo Vinciano (Leonardo's *Last Supper*), Piazza Santa Maria delle Grazie
☎ 02 4987588
🕐 Tue–Sat 9–7; Sun 9–8
Ⓜ M1 – Conciliazione
♿ Few
🍴 Expensive
❓ Booking a time to see the fresco is now obligatory.
☎ 199 199 100 for reservations

VILLA REALE ✪✪

Built in neo-classical style and once owned by Napoleon, the Villa Reale, standing at the edge of Milan's Public Gardens, is now the city's museum of modern art. The rooms are a marvel of 18th century elegance, with chandeliers, parquet floors and sumptuous plasterwork, to such an extent that the works, illustrating the artistic movements of the late 19th and early 20th centuries, can seem a little out of place. Many are by north Italian artists, but there are also paintings by Cézanne, Renoir, Gauguin, Picasso and Matisse. After exploring the museum, go to the back of the villa. The rear façade is by far the best and can be viewed across a delightful lake.

✚ 31E4
✉ Via Palestro 16
☎ 02 76002819
🕐 Daily 9:30–5:30
Ⓜ M1 – Palestro
♿ Few
🍴 Free

Villa Reale, Milan's museum of modern art

Milan highlights

Distance
2km

Time
1–3 hours, depending on museums visited

Start/End Point
In front of the Duomo in Piazza Duomo
✚ 31D2

The entrance to Galleria Vittorio Emanuele in Piazza Duomo

Lunch
Al Mercante (££)
✉ Piazza Mercanti 17
☎ 02 8052198
🕐 Closed Sunday

Museo del Duomo
✉ Piazzo Duomo
🕐 Daily 9:30–12:30, 3–6
☎ 02 860358
♿ Few
🎟 Moderate

Casa del Manzoni
✉ Via Morone 1
☎ 02 86460403
🕐 Tue–Fri and Sun 9–12, 2–4
♿ Few   🎟 Free

Start in front of the Duomo (► 18) in Piazza Duomo.

Facing the Duomo, bear right to walk along the side of the building. This is Via Arcivescovado, though you will not see this displayed. To the right is Palazzo Reale.

Palazzo Reale must not be confused with Villa Reale (► 33). It was once the Ducal Palace of the Viscontis and was partially destroyed by fire but renovated and added to over the years. Mozart's first opera was performed here when he was 14 years old. The *palazzo* houses the **Museo del Duomo**, a collection of religious artefacts.

Continue along the road, looking to the right at the church of San Gottardo with its beautiful campanile. Turn left behind the cathedral. To the right is the Palazzo Arcivescovile, built in 1170, while ahead is Piazza Fontana. At the end of the cathedral, turn left to return to the main square. Turn right through the Galleria Vittorio Emanuele.

Begun in 1865, the triumphal arch through which the walker passes completed the gallery's construction. The Milanese refer to the Galleria as *Il salotto di Milano*, the drawing room of Milan, because its cheap cafés and expensive restaurants are traditional meeting places. Look right to see the exclusive Savini's, where crowds assemble after the first night of operas at La Scala.

Exit the Galleria into Piazza della Scala. The opera house is to the left. Ahead is a statue of Leonardo da Vinci. Walk on, with Palazzo Marino to the right, then turn right to reach one side of the church of San Fedele. Step right into Piazza San Fedele.

San Fedele is the most complete of Milan's 16th-century churches. It was built by San Carlo Borromeo (► 43) and was once frequented by the Milanese elite. Outside is a monument to Alessandro Manzoni (► 14).

Regain the side of the church and bear left across the road to reach the Casa degli Omenoni.

Casa degli Omenoni is the House of Giants, after the eight caryatids sculpted on the outside by Leone Leoni for whom the house was built in 1565.

Continue past the House of Giants (along Via degli Omenoni), to reach Piazza Belgioioso, turning left along it.

Palazzo Belgioioso was built for a family whose name is carved in the piazza outside. Further on, to the left, is a museum in Manzoni's home from 1814 until his death.

Continue along Via Gerollamo Morone from the end of the square to reach Via Manzoni. Turn right towards the Poldi–Pezzoli Museum.

Housed in a fine 17th-century palazzo, this is one of Italy's foremost museums. Art includes *Profile of a Young Woman* by Pollaiolo and works by Luini, Mantegna and Botticelli. There are also antique clocks and ceramics.

Turn left along Via Manzoni, soon reaching Piazza della Scala again.

La Scala opera house was built in 1778, taking its name from the Scaligeri family, whose symbol was a ladder (*scala*). In its early days the theatre was mostly used as a gaming house but its reputation was transformed with the rise of Verdi. Today La Scala is one of the world's great opera houses. There is a small **museum** about the theatre.

Pass the theatre, crossing Via Santa Margherita, Via San Protaso and the tram lines of Via Tommaso Grossi. Go under the arch and across the pedestrianised road to Piazza dei Mercanti.

This beautiful little square is one of the gems of Milan. On the street side is the Palazzo della Ragione, its arcaded lower floor once a market, its upper storeys the town hall and law courts. Opposite is the Palazzo delle Scuole Palatine, a 17th-century school of mathematics, rhetoric and law, beside the 14th-century marble Loggia degli Osii.

Now take the few steps back to Piazza Duomo.

One of the giants of Casa degli Omenoni

Museo Poldi-Pezzoli
- ✉ Via Manzoni 12
- ☎ 02 794889
- 🕐 Tue–Sun 10–6. Early closing Sun afternoons (summer)
- ♿ Few
- 💵 Moderate

Museo Teatrale alla Scala
- ✉ Piazza della Scala
- ☎ 02 8879473
- 🕐 9–12, 2–5 (closed Sun Nov–Apr)
- ♿ Few
- 💵 Cheap
- ❓ The opera house closed in 2002 for refurbishment (expected to take 3 years). Operas will be staged in the Teatro degli Arcimboldi during the closure

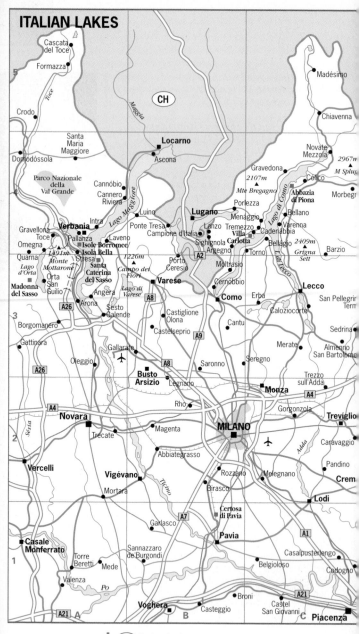

ITALIAN LAKES

Cascata del Toce
Formazza
Madésimo
Toce
Crodo
CH
Chiavenna
Santa Maria Maggiore
Locarno
Domodóssola
Ascona
Novate Mezzola
2967m
M Splug
Gravedona
Célico
Parco Nazionale della Val Grande
Cannóbio
2107m
Mte Bregagno
Abbazia di Piona
Morbegr
Cannero Riviera
Porlezza
Bellano
Luino
Lugano
Menággio
Verbania
Intra
Ponte Tresa
Lanzo
Tremezzo
Cadenábbia
Varenna
Gravellona Toce
Pallanza
Laveno
Campione d'Italia
Sighignola
Carlotta
Villa
Bellágio
2409m
Grigna
Omegna
Isole Borromee
Isola Bella
Santa
Argegno
Torno
Sett
Quarna
1491m
Monte Mottarone
Stresa
Caterina del Sasso
Porto Ceresio
Moltrasio
Barzio
Lago d'Orta
1226m
Campo del Fiori
Lecco
Madonna del Sasso
Orta San Giulio
Angera
Lago di Varese
Varese
Cernóbbio
Como
Erba
San Pellegrin
Term
A26
Arona
A8
Calozioorte
Sesto Calende
Castiglione Olona
Cantu
Borgomanero
Castelseprio
A9
Merate
Sedrina
Gattinara
Almenno
San Bartolome
A26
Gallarate
Oleggio
A8
Saronno
Seregno
Trezzo
sull'Adda
Busto Arsizio
Legnano
Monza
A4
Novara
Rho
Gorgonzola
Treviglio
A4
Trecate
Magenta
Caravaggio
Sesia
MILANO
Vercelli
Abbiategrasso
Pandino
Vigévano
Rozzano
Melegnano
Crem
Mortara
Birasco
Ticino
Adda
Lodi
Certosa di Pavia
A7
A1
Casale Monferrato
Garlasco
Pavia
Torre Beretti
Sannazzaro de Burgondi
Belgioioso
Casalpusterlengo
Mede
Codogno
Valenza
Po
Broni
A21
Voghera
Casteggio
Castel San Giovanni
Piacenza
A21
A

CH Switzerland

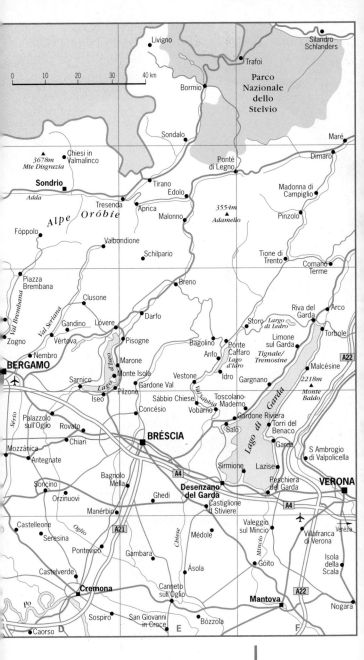

Western Lakes

Close to Mont Blanc there is a mountain peak (Mt Dolent) where France, Switzerland and Italy touch. From it the high ridge of the Alps heads north-westward and eastwards and the country borders follow it. The Matterhorn lies on the border between Switzerland and Italy, as does Monte Rosa. From Monte Rosa the high ridge and the border turn northeast towards the Simplon Pass. On the Italian side of the ridge the land falls away swiftly – it is barely 60km from the second highest summit in the Alps to the edge of the Lombardy Plain. This is the Italian region of Piemonte (Piedmont), a name which translates, accurately, as the foot of the mountains. The whole of Lake Orta and the western shore of Lake Maggiore lie within the region, the eastern shore lying in Lombardy.

> *'When a man has a heart and a shirt he should sell the shirt in order to see Lake Maggiore.'*

STENDHAL
The Memoirs of a Tourist,
1839

———————●———————

Looking across Lake Maggiore from Isola Bella

Lake Orta

By comparison to the lakes to the east, Orta is just a splash of water, yet at 14km long, almost 3km wide and 143m deep at its deepest point it would be a large lake in many other locations. The fall in altitude from Monte Rosa is such that Lake Orta sits at barely 300m above sea level – 4,300m below the summit of Monte Rosa which lies just 40km away. The steep drop in height levels out, Lake Orta being merely 100m above Lake Maggiore into which its outflowing stream eventually flows.

What to See around Lake Orta

ISOLA SAN GIULIO ✪✪✪

Visitors staying in Orta San Giulio (➤ 19) who rise with the sun and look out across the lake are sometimes treated to a rare sight. A thin, dense layer of mist lies on the water, waiting for just a little more sunlight before it rises and disperses, and above it, seemingly floating on a cloud, is Isola San Giulio. A similar, more easily observed but less striking view can be seen each night when buildings on the island are floodlit and seem disembodied against the dark waters of the lake and the mountains beyond.

On the island, the church dedicated to the founding saint is the finest Romanesque building in the area. Built in the 9th century on the site of San Giuilo's hermit cell, it contains many rare treasures. The black marble pulpit is 11th century, the carved lecterns and carved walnut choir stalls are masterpieces and a silver urn holds the remains of Giulio himself. There is also a section of bone from one of the dragons the saint displaced – though this is more probably a whale bone. Beside the church the 14th century Palazzo dei Viscovi is now a small monastery.

✚ 36A3
✉ Island off Orta San Giulio at the southern end of Lake Orta
🍴 Limited on the island, but lots of choice in Orta San Giulio (£–£££)
🚤 Reached by regular lake steamers or water 'taxis' from Orta San Giulio
♿ Reasonable on the island, difficult on all but the regular lake steamers

---

Right: *Lake Orta's western shore is edged with peaks*
Below: *Isola San Giulio seen from an approaching boat*

DID YOU KNOW?

Because of the lie of the land, the outflowing river from Lake Orta, the Torrente Nigoglia, which soon flows into the River Strona (which itself flows into the Toce to Lake Maggiore) flows north, towards the mountains, the only river in Italy to do so. This fact has been used by the locals to strike a blow for their independence from their neighbours: 'La Nigoglia goes up and we make the laws'.

OMEGNA ⭐
With a population of about 16,000, Omegna is Lake Orta's largest town. It is a pleasant place still retaining part of its 13th-century wall, though it is more industrialised than most of the other places on the lake. The ruins of an ancient bridge across the river still provoke debate between those experts who date its origins to the time when the town was Roman Vomenia, and those who detect more recent (but still medieval) work. Close to the lakefront is the town's old quarter, with some beautiful old houses, many still with their outside stairways and wrought ironwork, with balconies and shutters. Be sure to find time to visit the church of Sant'Ambrogio, which has an excellent 16th-century polyptych.

ORTA SAN GIULIO (► 19, TOP TEN)

THE WESTERN SHORE ⭐
Lake Orta's western shore is steep, the road which links the hillside villages narrow and twisting. But there are worthwhile places to visit. The highlight is the church of Madonna del Sasso perched on a granite outcrop close to the village of Boleto. The church, almost as big as some of the hamlets it overlooks, has some interesting artwork, including fine 18th-century frescoes and a 17th-century crucifix, but is most notable for the view from it which takes in virtually the entire lake.

Closer to Omegna are the upper and lower Quarna villages (Quarna Sopra and Quarno Sotto). The villages have a history of producing fine work in wood and brass and are particularly famous for making musical instruments. There is a small **museum of instruments** and their manufacture in Quarna Sotto, which is open during the summer months.

➕ 36A4

✉️ At the northern end of Lake Orta, straddling the lake's outflowing river

🍴 La Conchiglia, Via IV Novembre, 187 (££)

☎️ 032 362317

🚌 Buses from Gozzano and Gravellona Toce

 Regular lake steamers

♿ Reasonable

➕ 36A4

Museum of Musical Instruments

✉️ Quarna Sotto

☎️ 0323 826141

🕐 Aug daily 4–7. At all other times by request

🍴 Little locally, but a reasonable choice in Omegna

🚌 Infrequent buses from Omegna

♿ Few

💲 Cheap

Opposite: Part of the doll collection housed in Angera Castle

Lake Maggiore

As with Lake Lugano, visitors will find that to do a full circuit of the lake – a distance of 170km, rather too far to travel if justice is to be done to the places along the way – they will need to take their passports with them, as such a trip will cross into and out of Switzerland. The border crossings are usually very relaxed, but remembering the passport is critical just in case the Swiss let you in but the Italians are reluctant to return the favour later in the day. It is also worth taking insurance documents for your car as occasionally the border police will ask for them and have been known to turn back drivers without them around.

What to See around Lake Maggiore

ANGERA ✪✪

This small town tucked into a cove of Lake Maggiore's southeastern shore has a lovely lakefront walk shaded by chestnut trees. The **local museum** explores the town's interesting history, noting that Pietro Martire, the chronicler of Columbus's journey to the New World, was a local man. Though the town is pleasant, most visitors come to see the forbidding *rocca* (castle) that looms above it – visit the town by boat for a real appreciation of just how impressive and well sited this formidable fortress really is.

✚ 36A3
✉ At the southern end of Lake Maggiore's eastern shore
🍴 Bacco (££), Via Mazzini, 71 ☎ 0331 931319

Town Museum
✉ Via Marconi, Angera
☎ 0332 931133/391915
🕐 Mon, Thu, Sat 3–7
🎫 Free
🚌 Regular buses along the eastern shore
⛴ Regular lake boats

Castle and Doll Museum
✉ At top of steep hill from town, car or taxi essential
☎ 0332 931300
🕐 Mar–Nov daily 9:30–5:30 (4:40 in Oct and Nov)
🍴 None on site, but lots of choice in the town (£–££)
♿ Few
🎫 Cheap

The view across the lake from Arona is dominated by Angera Castle

It was built by the Borromean family in the 15th century and was cleverly designed to ensure that attacks invariably turned the attackers' unprotected right side towards the defenders. Inside it is unfurnished, its gaunt appearance adding to its sinister qualities, though some rooms have surprisingly subtle frescoes. The castle is now the home of an excellent **doll museum** which concentrates on European dolls from the 19th century to the present day.

ARONA

Standing across the lake from Angera, Arona owes its prosperity to the age of railways, as it stands at the point where the line from Switzerland through the Simplon Tunnel meets that which links Milan to Turin. This economically strategic position is reflected in the array of fine 19th-century houses. One older building, the Palazzo de Filippi, houses a **museum** which explores the town's history. There was a **castle** here too, its defenders staring across the lake at those in Angera's stronghold, but little now remains on the rocky outcrop above the town.

Just outside Arona stands the colossal **statue of San Carlo Borromeo**. The saint was born in Arona Castle in 1538, was appointed Cardinal at 22 and was Archbishop of Milan by the time he was 26. Though the fact that his uncle was Pope Pius IV may have helped his promotion, he was undoubtedly a devout and hard-working man. After his death a member of his family decided that Carlo deserved a memorial befitting his stature. The original idea envisaged 15 chapels surrounding a vast statue, though only three of these were begun and only one completed. The statue is 23.5m tall and stands on a 12m plinth.and is apparently a good likeness of the man, right down to his huge nose. At the time it was said that Carlo was too ugly to be anything except a saint. Visitors can climb up within for a precarious view from inside the head, but as the statue is made of bronze it can be stiflingly hot in high summer.

ISOLA BELLA (▶ 18, TOP TEN)

🞤 36A3

✉ At the southern end of Lake Maggiore's western shore

Town Museum

✉ Palazzo de Filippi, Arona
☎ 0322 242577
🕐 By request only
🍴 Pescatori (££), Via Marconi 27 C 032 248312
🚌 Infrequent buses along the western shore
🚤 Regular lake boats
♿ Few
💷 Cheap

Rocca di Arona (castle remains)

✉ Above the town to the west
☎ 0322 243601
🕐 Apr and May daily 2–5, Jun–Oct daily 10–7:30
🚌 No buses, so car or taxi required
♿ None
💷 Cheap

Statue of San Carlo Borromeo

✉ North of Arona
☎ 0322 242488
🕐 Daily 8:30–12:30, 2–6:30 (5 from Nov–Mar)
🚌 Regular buses along the western shore
🚤 Regular lake boats
♿ None
💷 Cheap

Borromean Islands

Off-shore from Stresa on Lake Maggiore's western shore lie three small islands. The most famous of these is Isola Bella (▶ 17), but the other two are also worth visiting.

ISOLA MADRE ✪

The largest island, and the one furthest from Stresa, is Isola Madre, the Mother Island. Here the Borromean family built a single villa, landscaping the parkland around it. The villa is decorated in a much more subdued and relaxed style than its neighbour on Isola Bella. The chapel beside it houses the tombs of many members of the Borromean family, reflecting the fact that Madre was a place where the family lived rather than where they impressed their rivals. The island's parkland is a treasure house of rare species including a Kashmir cypress, said to be the finest specimen in Europe. There are also rows of citrus plants scenting the air, and a tropical greenhouse.

ISOLA PESCATORI ✪✪✪

This, as the name implies, is the fisherman's island, the only one of the Borromean trio which reflects the original occupation of the islands. While the Borromeo family were transforming Isola Bella and laying claim to Isola Madre for their private villa, Pescatori was owned by the Archbishop of Novara, who refused to give it up. It is a marvellous place with fishing boats – the traditional *lucia* with which all visitors to the lakes soon become familiar – at the harbour edge and nets hung over the walls to dry in the sun. The island is entirely occupied by a village which is achingly picturesque and, apart from the area where boats drop visitors, free of souvenir shops. At the heart of the village is the 11th-century church with its neat conical spire.

✚ 36A4
✉ Off-shore from Stresa and Pallanza
☎ 0323 31261
🕐 Daily Mar–Oct 9–12:30, 1:30–5:30 (5 in Oct)
🍴 La Piratera (££), Isola Madre ☎ 032 331171
🚢 Regular lake boats from both Stresa and Pallanza
♿ Reasonable
💰 Expensive
❓ Visitors cannot land on the island unless they purchase an entry ticket

---

✚ 36A4
✉ Off-shore from Stresa
🍴 Unione (££), Via Lungo Lago C 0323 933798
🚢 Regular boats from Stresa
♿ Reasonable

Fishing boats at the harbour of Isola Pescatori

CANNERO RIVIERA ✪

Cannero was once described as the 'Genoese Riviera in miniature', a fact which prompted the town fathers to add Riviera to the name and to style itself as the 'Nice of Maggiore' because of the mildness of its winter climate. It was also described as 'a pearl in a bracket of villas and vineyards', a description that is much less appropriate today as the vineyards have all but gone. The villas remain, though: in one, Villa Sabbioncella, Garibaldi stayed after the battle of Luino during his Risorgimento campaign. Neither that villa nor any other is open to visitors, who must content themselves with an exploration of the huddle of narrow streets, each lined with fine houses. All explorations are likely to end at the little harbour from where there is a view of the two small Cannero or Malpaga islands, each of which is topped by the ruins of a castle. The castles date from the 12th century and were once occupied by a band of five brothers who terrorised the local villages and pirated any ship unfortunate enough to come too close. Eventually the Viscontis became fed up with this blatant display of lawlessness, though it took them six months to force the brothers out of their strongholds before destroying the castles.

✚ 36A4
⊠ On the western shore of Lake Maggiore to the north of Verbania
🍽 Al Ponte (£), Via Roma 19. ☎ 0323 788027
🚌 Regular bus service along the western shore
🚢 Regular lake steamers
♿ Reasonable

Many of Cannero Riviera's narrow streets are lined with fine old houses

DID YOU KNOW?

On 8 January 1522 a painting of the dead Christ, in the possession of a Cannobio innkeeper, began to weep blood from Christ's wounds. At the same time the town was spared from the plague. As a result of these and other miracles, the inn was demolished to make way for a chapel to house the miraculous painting, which still hangs, ornately framed, in the chapel.

CANNOBIO ✪

Though sadly split in two by the main road up Maggiore's western shore, Cannobio is still worth a visit. On the lakeside, narrow, picturesque streets lead to the Santuario della Pietà which houses the town's miraculous painting. The chapel is the work of Pellegrini, a famous 16th-century architect who was commissioned by San Carlo Borromeo himself, the two men's involvement an indication of the effect the miracle had on the area. On the mountain side of the main road, a minor road reaches the *orrido* of Sant'Anna. An *orrido* is a tight gorge through which a noisy stream rushes, in this case the Torrente Cannobio, which reaches the lake at the town. Close to the gorge is the neat church after which it is named.

✚ 36A4
⊠ The first town in Italy if travelling south from Switzerland along Lake Maggiore's western shore
🍽 Sant'Anna, at the orrido (££) ☎ 0323 70682
🚌 Infrequent bus service along the western shore
🚢 Regular lake steamers
♿ Reasonable

45

🚩 36A4

✉ On Lake Maggiore's
eastern shore

🚌 Infrequent buses along
lake's eastern shore

🚢 Regular lake steamers.
Car ferry (which takes
foot passengers) from
Verbania

Funivia

☎ 0332 668012

🕐 Apr–Sep daily 9:30–6
(Sat, Sun and holidays 7);
Oct–Mar Sat, Sun and
holidays 9:30–5

♿ None

👤 Moderate

🚩 36B4

✉ On lake Maggiore's
eastern shore

🚌 Infrequent buses along
lake's eastern shore

🚢 Regular lake steamers

🍴 Il Porticciolo, Via Fortino
40 (about 1.5km north)
(£££) ☎ 0332 667257

Town Museum

✉ Palazzo Verbania

☎ 0332 532057/543564

🕐 Mon 2–6:30, Sat 8:30–12

♿ Few

👤 Free

LAVENO ⭐⭐

Visitors who use the car ferry to cross Lake Maggiore from Verbania to Laveno are treated to a magnificent view of the town, which is dominated by the church of Santi Giacomo e Felipe, built only in the 1930s and on a very grand scale with a huge dome. Those arriving by boat will also note the curious yellow buckets which travel slowly up the hillside behind the town. The fact that Laveno has an industrial suburb – Mombello – might imply that these are part of a quarrying operation. In fact they are the trans-porters of one the lakes' area's most exciting *funivias*. Each of the buckets carries two people, and though the gate in is securely fixed there is no other protection. The exposure is no more than ordinarily terrifying, but the buckets do allow a good view of the brightly coloured butterflies that congregate along the swathe of scrub cut through the forest below the funivia. The view from Sasso del Ferro at the top is magnificent.

LUINO ⭐⭐

This delightful small town has two claims to fame. It was the first place in Italy to raise a statue in honour of Giuseppe Garibaldi, the hero of the Risorgimento. Garibaldi came to the town to raise another army after he had been defeated by the Austrians at the battle of Custozza. This event, and other aspects of the town's history, are explored in a **museum** in Palazzo Verbania. The statue stands in Piazza Garibaldi (of course) where, on Wednesdays, a market is held. The second claim is that the great artist Bernardino Luini was born here. A painting of the *Adoration of the Magi* in the church of San Pietro – at the eastern, uphill section of the town – is attributed by some experts to the artist. In the church of Madonna del Carmine beside the main lakeside road there are frescoes that are the work of pupils of Luini.

Left: *The vast church of Santi Giacomo e Felipe dominates Laveno*

DID YOU KNOW?

Alessandro Manzoni, a local pirate, was captured after a long reign of terror and sentenced to be hanged on the beach of Cerro del Lago Maggiore. His final request was a glass of wine but his executioners found there was no inn at Cerro. The pirate gave the village a look of disgust and turned to the hangman saying 'Better hell than this town of abstainers'.

Below: *Villa Taranto is famous for its spring tulip display*

PALLANZA ★

Pallanza is just one of three villages – the others are Intra and Verbania – which make up a complex usually known as Verbania. The other two villages form a semi-industrialised town and ferry port (Lake Maggiore's only car ferry links Verbania to Laveno), but Pallanza is sufficiently removed to maintain a degree of individuality.

The old village has the usual maze of narrow streets lined with fine houses. It has a long-standing reputation as an autumn and winter resort, and as a place where the flowers and shrubs seem to bloom even more colourfully than elsewhere. The latter led to the village being referred to as the 'cradle of flowers' in old guides to the lake. Pallanza as a resort is mentioned in the classic Hemingway book *A Farewell to Arms*, where the characters planned 'to go to Pallanza. It is beautiful there when, in autumn, the leaves change their colour....There is a nice village at Pallanza and you can row out to the islands where the fishermen live…'

Palazzo Dugnani, a fine 18th-century building in the old quarter, is now the **Museo del Paesaggio**, the museum of landscapes, with a collection of paintings and frescoes. The real treasure, however, lies just outside the village. **Villa Taranto**, a 16ha garden beside the road which links Pallanza with Verbania, is one of the world's great gardens. The villa is named after the Duke of Taranto, one of Napoleon's generals. He was an ancestor of Scotsman Neil McEachern, who renamed it when he bought the property early in the 20th century. McEachern created a garden of awesome splendour. It is criss-crossed by 8km of paths and has over 20,000 varieties of tree and shrub from all over the world. Some of these specimens are the only examples in Europe. There are also ponds and a greenhouse with rainforest plants. In spring the garden's Tulip Week, when over 80,000 tulips are in bloom, gathers crowds from all over the world. A little later, the blooming of the azaleas and rhododendrons is another highlight.

✚ 36A4
✉ Part of the Verbania complex of towns/villages on Lake Maggiore's western shore
🍴 Il Torchio, Via Manzoni 20 (££) ☎ 0323 503352
🚌 Infrequent buses along lake's western shore
🚢 Regular lake steamers

Villa Taranto
☎ 0323 404555
🕐 Gardens only Apr–Oct daily 8:30–6:30 or sunset
♿ Good
💷 Expensive

SANTA CATERINA DEL SASSO (➤ 22, TOP TEN)

STRESA ❀❀

Stresa is the most elegant of all Lake Maggiore's towns, its lakeside gardens speaking of a prosperity which is most definitely mirrored in the array of substantial hotels opposite. Of these hotels, the finest is the very grandly (if curiously) named Grand Hotel et des Iles Borromées, one of just two on the lakes which lie outside the star rating system because they are too luxurious merely to be five-star (the other is the Villa d'Este at Cernobbio on Lake Como). It was in this hotel that Hemingway had Frederick Henry stay to escape the war in *A Farewell to Arms*. It is interesting that for being so elegant and famous a centre – the town has a famous annual music festival and is frequently home to conferences and conventions – it is such a tiny place and has so few attractions within its boundaries. There are some good shops and the usual range of souvenir outlets; and Piazza Cadorna, the central square, with its pavement cafés is excellent, but that is all. The town is a fine centre for local excursions, though.

To the north is the lower station of the funivia to the Mottarone, from where there is a view of Monte Rosa. On clear days Milan's Duomo and the Matterhorn are visible.

The funivia makes a stop at the **alpine garden** near Gignese, where thousands of species of alpine flower have been planted since 1934. From the garden there is a splendid view of the lake. Beyond the funivia, Baveno is a very pleasant village with a 12th-century Romanesque façade and campanile. Beside the church is a baptistery with 15th-century frescoes. Baveno became a socialite resort after Queen Victoria stayed for a week in 1879. Southwards from Stresa is **Villa Pallavicino**. The 19th-century villa is not open to the public, but its 12ha parkland is. Here, there are formal gardens, but the most entertaining feature is the safari-style zoo, with the animals in minimal caging and good access for children to the more docile species.

✚ 36A4
✉ On Lake Maggiore's western shore
🍴 Piemontese, Via Mazzini 25 (££) ☎ 0323 30235
🚌 Infrequent buses along lake's western shore
⛴ Regular lake steamers.

Giardino Alpino
✉ Gignese
☎ 0323 61687
🕐 Apr–Oct Tue–Sun 9–5
♿ Reasonable
💲 Moderate

Villa Pallavicino
🕐 Mar–Oct daily 9–6
♿ Reasonable
💲 Moderate

Even in early spring Stresa is an attractive resort to visit

Swiss Lake Maggiore

The northern end of Lake Maggiore lies in Switzerland. Visitors who head north along the western shore will cross the border soon after leaving Cannobio. The first Swiss town to be reached is Ascona.

Ascona is a quiet and picturesque lake retreat

ASCONA ✪

Isadora Duncan, Herman Hesse and Paul Klee all spent time here, as did Lenin and Jung. The town's lakefront is traffic-free, allowing visitors to savour it in peace. Ascona is separated from the larger, better-known town of Locarno by the wide Maggia river. Those with time to spare can follow the Valle Maggia to reach Ponte Brolla from where the enchantingly named Val Centovalli – the Valley of a Hundred Valleys – leads off. This is fine walking country and is also followed by a railway.

⊞ 36B4
☒ Close to Locarno
🚌 Regular buses from Locarno
🚢 Regular lake steamers
♿ Reasonable

LOCARNO ✪✪✪

Locarno wraps itself around a sheltered inlet of the lake which, because it faces southwest and faces the lower hills, gets many hours of sunlight. The lakefront and nearby squares are alive with colourful flowers and pleasant pavement cafés. Inland from the lake, past the Kursaal Casino, the **Castello Visconti** is now a museum of local archaeology. At the heart of the old town is Piazza Grande, with its shops and restaurants. Heading north from it, along Via della Stazione, the lower station of a funivia is soon reached. This leads to the 15th-century church of Madonna del Sasso, with superb views of the lake and a cable-car, then a chairlift, rises to 1,672m. Elsewhere in the town, the Casa Rusca in Piazza Sant'Antonio, a fine 17th-century house, has a tradition of being occupied by artists, and holds regular exhibitions of work by contemporary painters and sculptors.

⊞ 36B4

Castello Visconti
☒ Locarno
☎ 091 7563186
🕐 Tue–Sun 10–12, 2–5
🍴 Villa Pauliska, Via Orselina 6 (££) ☎ 091 7430541
♿ Reasonable
💰 Moderate

Lake Lugano

Lugano is shaped like a fox, its long bushy tail and its head shared by Switzerland and Italy, its legs firmly anchored on Swiss soil. The city of Lugano and the northern shore of the lake were once part of the city state of Milan, but the Swiss took both the city and adjacent land in 1512. When Italy was freed from Austrian rule and unified, no claim was made on Milan's former territories and, despite the common language and the oddity of Campione, no serious attempt has ever been made to regain the northern shore. As a result, Italian Lake Lugano is fragmented: there is a small section of the south-western shore, the enclave of Campione and a larger section of the eastern lake. However, the lakesides in the east are steep and barely habitable with only Porlezza – at the head of the lake – being a reasonable size.

Santa Maria del Monte on Monte Campo dei Fiori above Varese

What to See around Lake Lugano

CAMPIONE D'ITALIA ✪✪

In the 8th century the local lord of this part of Lake Lugano gave in perpetuity the land which is now Campione to the church of Sant'Ambrogio in Milan. Remarkably, when the Swiss annexed Milanese holdings on the northern, and part of the southern, shores of the lake they respected the

✚ 36B4
✉ An Italian enclave on Lake Lugano's eastern shore

The Italian enclave of Campione lies beyond an imposing arch

original covenant and made no attempt to take the village which had grown up on the church's holding. During the struggles of Austrian rule over parts of north Italy and the wars of the Risorgimento, Switzerland made no attempt to absorb the village. And so, despite the fact that the village – which has now grown into a town – is entirely surrounded by Switzerland, it remains resolutely Italian. Of necessity, Campione uses the Swiss postal system and all the shops and restaurants accept Swiss money, but this is very much an Italian town. A scheme a few years ago to link the town with Italy by building a cable car from it to Sighignola, a small village near Lanzo d'Intelvi (► 62), failed when money and enthusiasm ran out. It is likely, therefore, that Campione's unique position, reachable only from Switzerland, will continue for many years. The town now makes the most of its position by having a **casino** that extracts the hard-earned cash of the Swiss who cross the lake from Lugano and further afield to enjoy its gaming tables and cabarets.

Visitors to Campione are left in little doubt about the unusual nature of the town when they are greeted by a huge arch and elaborate fountain, a distinctly ceremonial entranceway. Within the town be sure to visit the church of San Pietro. In medieval times the town was famous for the Maestri Campionesi, a group of architects, builders and sculptors who were renowned for the quality of their work. As with the more famous Maestri Comacina of Lake Como, the Campione group took pride in not revealing their individual names so no one person can be identified. The group built Sant'Ambrogio in Milan, Modena Cathedral and the more modest, but no less beautiful, church here.

🚍 Infrequent buses from Switzerland

🚢 Regular lake steamers

🍴 There is a restaurant in the casino, but those not visiting should try Da Candida, Via Marco 4 (££)
☎ 091 6497541

Casino

✉ Campione d'Italia

☎ 091 6401111

🕐 All year daily, restaurant open from 12 noon, gaming tables from 3PM

🎫 Good

❓ Lose as much as you can stand!

PONTE TRESA ✪

⊕ 36B4
✉ At the western end of Lake Lugano's southern shore

The bridge of the name crosses the Tresa river, the outflow of Lake Lugano flowing west to Lake Maggiore. The bridge, a five-arched, red granite structure, is also the border between Italy and Switzerland, and so there are actually two towns, both called Ponte Tresa. Italian Ponte Tresa is usually a traffic bottleneck, with lorries attempting to cross the border blocking the road through the village and causing chaos. If the visitor finds such a problem – and it is easy to spot as you enter the village from the Porto Ceresio side – the answer is to park early and to enjoy the lakefront on the eastern side of the village, a delightful area. The rest of the village is interesting for its shops, which carry a range of goods likely to appeal to the Swiss from across the bridge.

> ### DID YOU KNOW?
>
> Ponte Tresa can be the start point for a venture along the Swiss side of the Tresa river to reach Miglieglia and the lower station of a chairlift to Monte Lema. At 1,624m, the peak is a superb viewpoint for Lakes Lugano and Maggiore, and visitors can stand with one foot in Italy and the other in Switzerland.

PORTO CERESIO ✪✪

⊕ 36B3
✉ Close to the Swiss border on the southern shore of Lake Lugano

Porto Ceresio is one of the loveliest places on Lake Lugano

Following two sides of a square-cut bay of Lake Lugano, Porto Ceresio is a lovely place. The village is renowned for the views along the two arms of Lugano and across the lake to Morcote, but that is to ignore Porto Ceresio itself. There is nothing of great note here, just a huddle of pretty houses and the little harbour of the name, but it encapsulates the quiet elegance of the older, less 'touristy' lakes. From the village a road heads south towards Varese, soon reaching Besano, a village famous for the local rocks, which are one of Italy's most important sources of Triassic

fossils – there is a small **fossil museum**. Further along, the same road leads to Bisuchio, where the 16th-century **Villa Cicogna Mozzoni** is a national monument. The villa has an arcaded ground floor, important frescoes and stands in Italian-style gardens.

VARESE AND SURROUNDINGS

The large, modern city of Varese is built on flat land below Monte Campo dei Fiori. It is a prosperous place, famous for its shoe making, but with other light industries and a reputation as a 'garden city' because of its parks and the lushness of the local valleys.

Within the city, which is worth visiting for its wealth of modern shops, be sure to see Del Bernascove, the 72m-high campanile that stands at the heart of the old town and is a symbol of Varese. There is an interesting complex of religious buildings beside the campanile. One, the 12th-century baptistery of San Giovanni, is a national monument. Near by, the baroque Palazzo Estense is another national monument. It was built by Francesco II Este, Duke of Modena, in the mid-18th century, is fronted by formal gardens, but stands in an extensive natural park.

From Varese, Monte Campo dei Fiori can visited for a view of the picturesque village of Santa Maria del Monte, or the local lakes and valleys can be explored. Lake Varese is the largest of the three lakes between the city and Lake Maggiore. On the lake's island, Isolina Virginia, excavations have revealed prehistoric remains of enormous importance. Of the valleys, the Valganna, which takes the main road to Ponte Tresa, is the most scenic, with small lakes and fine woodland, but the Valcuvia – between Varese and Lake Maggiore – is the most interesting. From it a side road climbs steeply to **Arcumeggia**, where, from the 1950s, contemporary artists have frescoed the outside walls of the houses to create an open-air art gallery. The works are not of the highest quality perhaps, but the idea is great fun.

South of Varese, Castiglione Olona should be visited to see one of Lombardy's most important **complexes of medieval buildings**. In the early 15th century Cardinal Branda Castiglioni, a local man, built a palazzo for himself, a house for his parents, a beautiful domed church, a baptistery and a collegiate church – the churches and baptistery being frescoed by the master artist Masolino de Panicale. There is a small museum devoted to the history of the site.

Museo Paleontologico
- ⊠ Via Prestini, Besano
- 🕐 Sun 10–12, 4–6
- 🚌 Buses from Varese
- ♿ Few
- 🎟 Cheap

🚩 36B3

Arcumeggia
- ⊠ At top of steep road from the Valcuvia; car or taxi essential, but parking can be difficult
- ☎ 0332 283604
- ♿ None, but streets are reasonable

One of the frescoes at Arcumeggia

Church Complex/ Museum
- ⊠ Castiglione Olona. On the N233 (Milano) road south of Varese
- ☎ 0331 858048/858301
- 🕐 Tue–Sun 9–12, 3–6
- 🍴 Colombo Rosella (££), Via Cesare Battisti 112, Castiglione Olona
    - ☎ 0331 859275
- 🚌 Infrequent buses
- ♿ Few
- 🎟 Moderate

Swiss Lake Lugano

A large portion of Lake Lugano lies in the Swiss canton of Ticino. Here visitors can easily spend a day or two exploring the elegant, modern city of Lugano, and the lovely scenery and towns near by.

36B4

Museo Cantonale d'Arte
✉ Lugano
☎ 091 9104780
🕐 Wed–Sun 10–6, Tue 2–6; closes at 5 in winter
♿ Reasonable
✋ Moderate

Villa Favorita
✉ Lugano
☎ 091 9716152
🕐 Apr–Oct Fri–Sun 10–6, Tue 2–6
♿ Good
✋ Moderate

Steamers often cross the Swiss-Itallian border on Lake Lugano

LUGANO ✪✪

Most of Lugano's highlights lie close to the lake. At the southern end of the city is Paradiso, a suburb of new hotels, good restaurants, nightclubs and shops. Heading north, the visitor is soon in the old quarter of the city with its narrow streets and large open squares. Here, the church of Santa Maria Degli Angioli has frescoes by Bernardino Luini, pupil of Leonardo and, some maintain, the equal of his master. The paintings are some of Luini's best. From Piazza Luini, in which the church stands, follow Via Nassa north. The surrealist sculpture in Piazzetta San Carlo is *The Dignity of Time* by Salvador Dalí. Via Nassa leads to Piazza della Riforma, with its cafés and the impressive town hall. The square is one of the main venues for Lugano's famous Jazz Festival each June. Cross to the lakeside and continue towards Parco Civico. Inland from here is Quartière Maghetti, a modern district of shops and restaurants. On the edge of the Quartière is a **gallery of contemporary art** which holds regular exhibitions showing the work of all Swiss, but chiefly Ticino, artists. The city's more famous art collection is housed in **Villa Favorita** further along the lake. Until recently, this housed the Thyssen-Bornemisza collection of paintings, one of the best private collections in the world. The bulk of the collection is now in Madrid, but what remains is still impressive. The Villa also holds regular exhibitions.

Lugano's Parco Civico is an excellent place for a lakeside stroll

EAST OF LUGANO ✪✪

From Lugano a funicular climbs **Monte Bré**, to the north. The peak is renowned not only for its view and as a starting point for walks, but as a sun trap. Another funicular, from Paradiso, reaches **Monte San Salvatore**, where the view includes not only the lake and the city, but the Valais Alps and the Bernese Oberland.

To the east of Lugano, at Gandria, a fascinating **museum** explores the work of the Swiss customs and the ingenious methods used by smugglers to bring contraband in and out of Switzerland. The most bizarre item is a submarine whose torpedo tubes were filled with salami.

SOUTH OF LUGANO ✪✪

Heading south from Lugano there are several interesting places on the northern shores of the lake. At Melide, the **Swissminiatur** is a replica of all the main sites in Switzerland set out on a 1ha site. From Melide a funivia takes visitors to Carona where there is a fine park and a church with 16th-century frescoes. Further on, Morcote is often called the 'Pearl of the Lake'. With its narrow streets of arcaded houses and the beautiful setting of the church of Santa Maria del Sasso among tall cypresses, it is easy to see why. Elsewhere on the peninsula of land which ends at Morcote, admirers of the writing of Herman Hesse can make a pilgrimage to Gentilino where he is buried.

Further from Lugano, and across the lake, at Capolago, a **rack railway** takes visitors to the top of Monte Generoso, a much higher peak, with more expansive views. From the top, walkers can explore an alpine landscape rich in wildflowers.

✚ 36B4

Museo Doganale Svizzero (Smuggling Museum)

✉ Gandria

☎ 091 9239843

🕐 Daily Easter–Oct 2:30–5:30

🍴 Limited locally, but there is a good choice in Lugano

♿ Good

🎫 Moderate

✚ 36B4

Swissminiatur

✉ Melide

☎ 091 6401060

🕐 Daily mid-Mar to Oct 9–6

🍴 There is a café at the site

♿ Good

🎫 Moderate

Rack Railway to Monte Generoso

✉ Capolago

☎ 091 6481105

🕐 Daily May–Oct 10–6 or dusk

🍴 Café at the top (£)

♿ Few

🎫 Expensive

Lake Como & the Bergamo Valleys

Once a glacier filled the valleys that now carry the Adda and Mera rivers. It flowed south, bumping against the vast triangle of rock that now underlies the High Brianza, its tip at the Punta Spartivento (near Bellagio). The rock of the triangle was hard, splitting the glacier and deepening two valleys to create a lake which is an inverted Y, the points of its arms at Como and Lecco. Interestingly, the Lecco arm lies a little higher than the Como arm so that the lake flows through the Adda, which flows past Lecco. There is no outlet on the Como arm and when rain increases the lake's volume beyond that which can be easily taken by the Adda the lake overflows, occasionally flooding Piazza Cavour, the lakeside square in Como.

Lake Como is the most elegant of all the lakes with an array of fine towns, villas and gardens to delight the visitor.

> *'I ask myself 'Is this a dream ?*
> *Will it all vanish into air ?*
> *Is there a land of such supreme*
> *And perfect beauty anywhere ?''*

HENRY LONGFELLOW
By Sommariva's Garden Gate
(Sommariva was the second owner of Villa Carlotta)

●

Lake Como is renowned for its pretty villages and stunning mountain scenery

Como's cathedral displays a fusion of architectural styles

 36B3

Como

Como occupies an ancient site that has been inhabited since at least the Bronze Age. During the Roman period Julius Caesar himself brought 5,000 Greeks to settle in the town, the start of its rise to prosperity. After the fall of Rome, Como was the home of the Maestri Comacina, a group of architects, builders and sculptors whose work is still admired today. The disastrous Ten Years War with Milan ruined the town, but it recovered and became a centre for wool and silk industries, the latter still being carried on here.

What to See in Como

 36B3
✉ Piazza Duomo

BROLETTO ✪✪

Piazza Duomo lies just a few steps inland from Piazza Cavour and the lake. As you enter the square, the first building on your left is the Broletto, the 13th-century town hall. It has an arcaded ground floor with triple-arched windows above, and is attached to a tall campanile.

 36B3
✉ Piazza Duomo
🍴 Imbarcadero (£££), Piazza Cavour 20 ☎ 031 270166 or La Colonne (££), Piazza Mazzini 12 ☎ 031 266166.

DUOMO ✪✪✪

Dominating Piazza Duomo is the west façade of the cathedral, a masterpiece of Gothic architecture with statues peering out from its niches. The façade dates from the 15th century, but the Duomo took many years to complete and shows a distinct range of styles. The eastern end mixes Gothic and Renaissance and the dome was

DID YOU KNOW?

On 28 February 1745 Alessandro Volta was born at 10 Contrada di Porta Nuova, Como (though the house was later renumbered 62). Despite not having a formal training in physics, Volta published important papers on electricity and magnetism by the time he was 20. Volta was a schoolmaster in Como at first, but was made Professor of Physics at Padua University in 1778. After retirement he returned to Como where he died in 1827. He is remembered in the town at the impressive Tempio Voltiano where some his experimental equipment is displayed, together with other memorabilia. An electrical unit, the volt, is named after Volta.

added only in the 18th century. The oldest section of the building was the work of the Rodari brothers and it was they who carved the exquisite south door and the Porta della Rana, the Frog door, on the north side, so called because there is a frog carved on one pillar. Inside, the Duomo is sombre, but has some good artwork, including paintings by Bernardino Luini.

During a walk around the town, a good coffee stop is Caffè Greco, Via Vittorio Emanuele 48 ☎ 031 262147

PORTA VITTORIA ✪

At the far end of the old town from the lake is a tall, sturdy tower built in the 12th century to protect one of the gates through the old wall. During the wars of the Risorgimento Garibaldi defeated an Austrian army under Marshall Urban at nearby San Fermo and marched in triumph through Porta Vittoria.

 36B3
✉ Via Cantú/Piazza Vittoria

SANT'ABBONDIO AND SAN CARPOFORO ✪✪

These two fine basilicas, both the work of the Maestri Comacina, are named after early Christians who preached in the Como area. With its severe façade and twin towers, Sant'Abbondio is now recognised as one of the great masterpieces of the Lombard Romanesque style. Inside, it has rows of elegant columns and superb 14th-century frescoes which illustrate the life of Christ.

San Carpoforo is thought to occupy the site of a Roman temple to Mercury, but has a Christian tradition which is at least 1,500 years long. The exterior is similar to that of Sant'Abbondio, but inside it is a complete contrast, with elegant steps and unfrescoed walls.

Sant'Abbondio
 Via Sant'Abbondio

San Carpoforo
✉ Via Brenta

SAN FEDELE ✪✪✪

San Fedele is the finest of Como's trio of churches built by the Maestri Comacina. Standing in Piazza San Fedele, at the centre of the old town, it is a wonderful building, though to see the very best work, go out of the square and around the church. Inside, the frescoes, dating from the 14th to the 16th centuries, are breathtaking.

 36B3
 Piazza San Fedele

In the Know

If you only have a short time to visit the Italian Lakes and would like to get a real flavour of the region, here are some ideas:

10
Ways to Be a Local

Buy a mobile phone. No local is seen without one and rarely seen not using it.

Learn to talk with your hands and body. Unless you master the full range of shrugs and arm waves you will never speak Italian.

Buy a scooter. The Italians have both the climate and the enthusiasm for scooter riding.

Learn to eat spaghetti. None of that nonsense with spoon and fork, they do it with fork alone and never have long ends that need to be messily sucked up.

Drink *liscio*. The Italians drink coffee thick, strong and black – an acquired taste.

For him – buy a whole new

Learn to talk with your hands

wardrobe and learn how to wear it. No one in Italy is scruffy; even in jeans and a T-shirt the Italian is the height of fashionable elegance.

For her – the same fashion sense resides in the Italian woman, but to really be a local you should also have your hair elegantly styled and spend time each day maintaining it.

Get a bicycle. The Italians have the healthy habit of cycling regularly on a Sunday, always dressed in clothing that would do justice to a Giro rider.

Buy some sunglasses. The sun warrants the wearing of sunglasses, but fashion requires them too, the trendier the better.

Learn to relax. Northern Italy is the economic heart of the country, but the locals are not only hard

working – they know how to relax too, taking leisurely lunches and evening strolls.

10
Top Places to have Lunch

Da Candida (££)
✉ Via Marco 4, Campione d'Italia ☎ 091 6497541

Al Mercante (££)
✉ Piazza Mercanti 17, Milan ☎ 02 8052198

La Laconda dell'Isola (££)
✉ Isola Comacina
☎ 0344 56755

Il Porticciolo (£££)
✉ On the lakeside road about 2km south of Laveno
☎ 0332 667257

Sacro Monte (££)
✉ Via Sacro Monte 5
☎ 0322 90220

Bilacus (££) ✉ Via Serbelloni 32, Bellagio
☎ 031 950480

Shopkeeper in Orta St Giulio taking it easy

**Colleoni e Dell'Angelo
(£££)** ✉ Piazza Vecchia 7,
Bergamo (Upper City)
☎ 035 232596
Olevo (££) ✉ Piazza Bra
18, Verona ☎ 045
8030598
Unione (££) ✉ Via Lungo
Lago, Isola dei Pescatori
☎ 0323 933798
Touring (£)
✉ At Sighignola, near
Lanzo d'Intelvi
☎ 031 840688/840692

10
Top Activities

- Birdwatching (➤ 12–13)
- Climbing (➤ 114)
- Sailing (➤ 114)
- Skiing (winter) (➤ 114)

- Swimming (➤ 114)
- Taking a boat ride
- Walking (➤ 114)
- Waterskiing (➤ 114)
- Windsurfing (➤ 114)
- Wildflower hunting
(➤ 12–13)

10
Top Souvenirs

- Artworks
- Fashionwear
- Handbags
- Handicrafts
- Jewellery
- Olive oil
- Shoes
- Silk scarves for her
- Silk ties for him
- Wines (Bardolino or
Valpolicella)

5
Great Rides

- The rack railway to
Monte Generoso (➤ 55)
- The bucket lift to
Sasso del Ferro from
Laveno (➤ 46)
- The cable-car to Monte
Baldo (➤ 86)
- The funivia to Brunate
from Como
- The cable-car to the
Mottarone from Stresa
(➤ 48)

5
Top Views from
the Lakes

- The town of Bellagio
(➤ 16)
- The church of Santa
Caterina del Sasso
(➤ 22)
- The town and castle of
Malcesine (➤ 86)
- The town of Sirmione
(➤ 23)
- Isola San Giulio
(➤ 40)

5
Great Views from
above the Lakes

- Lake Lugano from
Sighignola (➤ 62)
- Lake Maggiore from
the Mottarone (➤ 48)
- Lake Garda from
Tignale/Tremosine
(➤ 24)
- Lake Como from Pigra
(➤ 63)
- Lake Orta from
Madonna del Sasso

*The lakes' mild climate
make them perfect for
alfresco eating*

The Intelvi Valley

Distance
105km

Time
4–5 hours

Start/End point
The lake front, Como
⊞ 36B3

Lunch
Touring (£)
⊞ Sighignola
☎ 031 840688/840692

*View from Sighignola:
below the clouds lies
Lake Lugano*

In Como, follow the road with the lake to your right, past traffic lights, then right on the road to Switzerland. At the top of the hill turn right, back towards the lake, then take the road which bypasses the lakeside villages. Near Argegno, turn left for Schignano/Erbonne/Cerano.

Schignano is not a single village but a collection of scattered hamlets. Erbonne lies at the end of a long road and is set just a short distance below the Swiss border. In the centre of the village is the old communal wash house.

Wind uphill for lovely views of the lake. Go through S. Anna and follow the signs for Casasco, through Schignano, to the boundary sign for Cerano d'Intelvi. Pass the church, then turn left for Casasco/San Fedele/Veglio.

Follow this bumpy road to a junction and turn right. At the next T-junction, in San Fedele d'Intelvi, turn left along a road signed for Lanzo, Porlezza and Switzerland.

The road improves now, passing the twin villages of Pello d'Intelvi (Inferiore and Superiore). Go through Scaria to reach Lanzo, then bear right at the Hotel Milano for the funivia down to Santa Margherita, an Italian village on Lake Lugano's southern shore. Return to Hotel Milano and bear right for Sighignola. Past Lanzo d'Intelvi, drive along Via Sighignola, climbing through pretty woods to reach Sighignola itself.

At Sighignola, there is a fabulous viewpoint and an uncompleted funivia to Campione d'Italia. Enjoy the magnificent view of Lake Lugano, Monte Rosa and the Alps before reversing the drive to Lanzo.

In the square, bear right – with the Cristal Bar to your left – to reach a junction. Turn left, then right shortly after, for Como, going through Castiglione d'Intelvi and descending to the lake at Argegno. Turn right to return to Como.

Argegno's lakefront is ideal for a quiet hour's fishing

What to See around Lake Como

ARGEGNO

Argegno is a pretty town, best seen from the road which descends from the Intelvi villages (► 62), when the red-tiled roofs of the houses stand out against the wooded valley of the Telo river and the lake. The view from the lakefront is superb, with a long arm of the lake in both directions and, northwards, the mountains above Varenna, snow-capped in winter. To make the best of the view, go just a little out of town to the north and take the funivia to Pigra, well-known not only as viewpoint but for the profusion of wildflowers that grow near the top station.

🚑 36B4
✉ On Lake Como's western shore
🍴 La Griglia, 1 Fraz Sant'Anna (£) ☎ 031 821147
🚌 Regular buses from Como
🚢 Regular lake steamers
♿ Reasonable

BELLAGIO (► 16, TOP TEN)

BELLANO

On the lake front of Bellano there are memorials to the 19th-century writer Tommaso Grossi and the 17th-century scientist Sigismondo Boldoni. Neither of the pair is very well known outside Italy, but Bellano is proud of its famous sons. It is also proud of the fact that it was another member of the Boldoni family, Pietro, who introduced the silk industry to Como. The old quarter of the town is extremely attractive, but most visitors come to see the *orrido*, the gorge of the Pioverna stream, which is arguably the finest of its kind in the lakes area. Spring's melting snow swells the stream, the extra volume having cut a deep narrow gorge through the rocks above the town. A series of ladders and walkways allows the visitor to explore the gorge: when the stream level is high the spray and constant hammering of the water make this an exciting journey.

🚑 36C4
✉ On Lake Como's eastern shore
🍴 La Darsena, Via Alberto 8 (££) ☎ 0341 810317
🚌 Regular buses along the eastern shore from Lecco
🚢 Regular lake steamers
♿ Reasonable

In the Grigna

Distance
12km, but involving 1,000m of climbing

Time
5–6 hours

Start/end point
Vo di Moncodena
🚩 36C4

Lunch
Rifugio Brioschi
✉ On the summit of the Grignone
☎ 0341 910498

The summit of Grigna Settentrionale is marked with a cross

To reach the start, drive to Esino Lario and take the road for Cainallo, continuing to Vo di Moncodena, and park.

Follow the red and yellow paint splashes and occasional route numbers (Route 25). After about 30 minutes you will reach a fork: continue along Route 25, an undulating track that leads to another fork. Go right onto Route 24, through woodland. Then the path hugs the steep rocky face to the left to reach the Porta Prada.

The Porta Prada is a natural rock arch that has a crucifix within it. Beyond the arch, the path is occasionally devious as it crosses steep ground, but is always obvious: continue along it to reach Rifugio Bietti where food and drink are available in the summer.

Go behind the hut and attack the steep slope ahead along a zigzag path. At the top you emerge on to a ridge: go right along the obvious path. Close to the summit the ground steepens and a chain offers extra purchase, but it is not dangerous if care is taken. Eventually you will scramble on to level ground, where a chapel has been built astride the ridge. Go past this and up the last few metres to the hut Rifugio Brioschi.

The hut is almost at the summit of Grigna Settentrionale, at 2,409m the highest point of the Grigna range. It is known locally as the Grignone (Big Grigna) and is marked with a cross. To the south is Grigna Meridionale, a 2,148m summit which is known as Grignetta (Little Grigna). To the south is the Lombardy Plain, while to the west and north are high peaks, including Monte Rosa and the Matterhorn.

Return along the ascent route, past the chain, but at its end take the path ahead rather than the ridge path. This becomes more difficult lower down, but the way is always downhill and walkers eventually reach the Rifugio Bogani . From the hut, follow Route 25 across the final face of the Grigna to reach the fork on the outward path where we branched right. Now reverse the outward walk back to the start.

CADENABBIA ⭐

Visitors heading north along the western shore of Lake Como beyond Argegno reach Sala Comacina and the start of the Zocca dell'Oli, the Olive Hollow, every spare piece of land having an olive grove. Beyond Ospedaletto's famous campanile are Tremezzo and Villa Carlotta (► 16), then Cadenabbia. The lake is at its widest here, attaining this full width just beyond Bellagio's Punta Spartivento. That position, which minimises the shading of the Grigna and the peaks of the High Brianza, explains the array of fine villas in and above the village. Verdi stayed in one while finishing his score for La Traviata. The village's position also explains why it is a terminus for Como's main car ferry, linking Cadenabbia with Bellagio and Varenna.

🔲 36C4
✉ On Lake Como's western shore
🍴 The best locally is La Figurida (£) in Rogaro Ovest near the village ☎ 0344 40676
🚌 Regular buses along the lake's western shore
⛴ Regular lake steamers and car ferries link to Varenna and Bellagio
♿ Reasonable

CERNOBBIO ⭐⭐

Cernobbio is a small industrial town, though it has a fine old quarter and an excellent lakefront. At the northern edge of the town is Villa d'Este, built in the 16th century for Cardinal Tolomeo Gallio, Secretary of State to Pope Gregory XIII. No expense was spared, and it's claimed that the villa today looks much as it did when the cardinal took possession of it. Over the years the villa has seen some of the richest and most powerful of Europe's elite. It was named by Caroline, estranged wife of George Frederick, later King George IV of Britain. Believing herself to be descended from the Este family of Ferrara, Caroline altered the villa's name. The villa's gardens include a curious stepped double waterfall which flows across a bridge over the lakeside road from Cernobbio to Moltrasio, and a series of castellated lookouts carved into the rock face. Today, the villa is a luxury hotel that boasts a floating swimming pool, unique in Italy.

🔲 36B3
✉ On Lake Como's western shore
🍴 Harry's Bar (£), Piazza Risorgimento 2 ☎ 031 512647
🚌 Infrequent buses along the western shore from Como
⛴ Regular lake steamers
♿ Reasonable

A flower-filled lucia *(fishing boat) at Cernobbio*

✚ 36C4

🍴 Lauro (£), Via Tagliaferri
12, Gravedona ☎ 034
485255 or Spinnaker (£),
Via Calozzo, Pianello del
Lario ☎ 034 487219

🚌 Regular buses along the
western shore

⛴ Regular lake steamers

**Museo 'La Raccolta
della Barca Lariana'
(Boat Museum)**

✉ Pianello del Lario
☎ 0344 87235/87294
🕐 Apr–Oct Sat and Sun
10:30–12:30, 2:30–6:30.
Daily Jul to mid-Sep
2:30–6:30
💰 Moderate

*Taking a break on the
lakefront at Domaso*

GRAVEDONA

Gravedona is a good centre for exploring the northern
section of Lake Como's western shore. In medieval times
the town was the senior partner of the Tre Pievi – the
Three Parishes, the other two being Dongo and Sorico –
which maintained its independence of the city states to
the south. The Tre Pievi occasionally supplemented trade
with piracy, using a ship with a golden crucifix attached to
the prow, which the villagers claimed made it invincible.
Once the ship attacked and defeated a treasure ship of the
Emperor Frederick I (the feared Barbarossa – 'Red Beard').
The Emperor was outraged, but the gold was to support
his campaign against the Lombard League and after his
defeat at the battle of Legnano in 1176 he was forced to
make concessions in the Treaty of Constance in 1183.
Some of those concessions were to the Tre Pievi.

Gravedona has some fine buildings. The town council
now occupies the 'Villa of Delights' of Cardinal Tolomeo
Gallio (who also owned Villa d'Este at Cernobbio ► 65),
while the 12th-century church of Santa Maria del Tiglio,
which was built on the site of a 5th-century baptistery, still
shows sections of the mosaic flooring of the original.

South of Gravedona, at Pianello del
Lario, an interesting **museum** housed
in an old mill explores the development
of boats and boat building on the lake,
while to the north, the pretty village of
Domaso is renowned as the best place
on Lake Como for windsurfing because
of the dependable winds.

DID YOU KNOW?

When Mussolini was thrown from
power, he and several other Fascist
leaders were hidden in a German
convoy along Lake Como, escaping
to Austria. At Dongo the convoy was
stopped by Italian partisans. The
Fascists were held in Palazzo Monti,
now Dongo's town hall. Thirteen
were tried and executed. Mussolini
and Clara Petacci were driven south
but at Azzano the partisan leader
decided that Italy's dignity would be
damaged by a trial of the former
Duce. The pair were shot at once.

A Ferry Ride from Como

To see one of the most interesting attractions on Lake Como, and to get a glimpse of another, it is necessary to use the lake steamers.

The island of Comacina is passed by steamers on the lake

At Como, the boats leave from the edge of the road which runs past Piazza Cavour, giving an old-world charm to the departure. Note that the itinerary of the boats varies, not all of them visiting the smaller villages. The trip starts by crossing to Cernobbio, where the quay is an elegant timber walkway to a refined waiting room and ticket office. On the next leg the boat offers a marvellous view of Villa d'Este, which is difficult to see from the road.

Beyond Cernobbio the ferry will call at several of the little villages on both the east and west shores of the lake – Blevio, Moltrasio, Torno, Urio, Carate and Faggeto Lario. On the eastern shore, between Torno and Faggeto Lario, stands Villa Pliniana, which can only be seen from the lake. Its position means that it gets only afternoon sun, and little of that in winter, so that it has gained a reputation as gloomy, even sinister. Yet the villa is a lovely building and has been visited by far from gloomy guests. Byron, Stendhal and Liszt all stayed and Rossini composed *Tancredi* here. The name commemorates a local well in which the water rises and falls apparently by magic.

*The ferry stops a few more times before reaching Argegno. It then rounds Isola Comacina and then passes the **Villa del Balbianello**, which can only be reached, or even seen, from the water.*

Though built as a *palazzo*, Villa del Balbianello became a rest home for Franciscan monks,. A statue of St Francis greets those arriving at the quay. Today, the villa is open to visitors, who must take a boat from Lenno or Campo.

The ferry usually stops at Lenno and Tremezzo, but the final highlight soon appears – the view of Bellagio as the ferry nears the village. Return from Bellagio is either by boat or by bus.

Distance
About 30km in a direct line, but probably 50km because the ferry criss-crosses the lake.

Time
Depends on the number of stops. If the *aliscafo* – hydrofoil – is taken it is only 45 minutes from Como to Bellagio (or return). On a conventional boat, which stops at most of the little villages this can rise to 2 hours.

Start/End point
Como
🚩 36B3

Lunch
Bilacus (££)
✉ Via Serbelloni 32, Bellagio
☎ 031 950480

Villa del Balbianello
☎ 0344 56110 or 02 4676151
🕐 Garden only Apr–Oct Tue and Thu–Sun 10–12:30, 3:30–6:30. Villa open by request only
🚢 From Lenno or Campo
♿ Few
💶 Moderate

🔲 36C3
✉ At the southern tip of
Lake Como's eastern arm
🚌 Regular buses from
Como
🚢 Regular lake steamers
🍴 Cermenati, Corso
Matteotti 71 (££)
☎ 0341 283017

Villa Manzoni
✉ Via Amendola
☎ 0341 481249
🕐 Tue–Sat 10–12:30,
2:30–5:30
♿ Reasonable
🎫 Moderate

Palazzo Belgioioso
✉ Corso Matteotti
☎ 0341 481249
🕐 Tue–Sat 10–12:30,
2:30–5:30
🚌 Regular buses from
Como
♿ Few
🎫 Moderate

LECCO ★★
There is a good deal of rivalry between Lecco and Como.
The cities are about equal in size, and while Como is more
historically interesting (and, most unbiased observers
would maintain, more elegant), Lecco is without doubt
more dramatically sited, beside the lake's only outflow
river and below the steep cliffs of Monte Coltignone to the
northwest, and the Resegone to the east. Though the
Como arm of the lake and its single northern reach are part
of Lake Como, it would be a brave person who would not
refer to the eastern arm as Lake Lecco when staying in the
town. Piani d'Erna, a popular walking area beneath the
Resegone, is reached by a cable car from Versasio above
the town and offers a splendid view of the Lecco and lake.

The town lies entirely on the lake's eastern shore and is
reached from the west by two bridges that span the Adda.
The furthest of these from the lake is Ponte Visconti, built
on the orders of Azzone Visconti in 1336. The original
bridge had drawbridge sections at each end. When it was
renovated to look as it had done on construction, its 11
arches were maintained, but plans stopped short of repro-
ducing the drawbridges. In Piazza XX Septembre, the Torre
Visconti is another reminder of Milanese influence. A
market has been held in the square below the tower since
at least 1149. Elsewhere, there is a fine statue of

DID YOU KNOW?

Pliny the Elder's *Natural History* claims that the waters
of the River Adda flow the entire length of the lake
without mixing with lake water.

Above: *Seen from the
south, Lecco is framed by
high limestone peaks*

Alessandro Manzoni, Lecco's famous son (► 14), and his childhood home is now a **museum** with a collection of memorabilia. The town's tourist office also produces a leaflet identifying places mentioned in Manzoni's book *The Betrothed*. Most of the sites are actually in Olate, a village above and east of the town. To the north of Villa Manzoni, and also worth visiting, is **Palazzo Belgioioso**, a 17th-century mansion which now houses the town's museum.

MENAGGIO ✪

Menaggio's position, halfway along the western shore of Lake Como, where an easy route links the Como valley to the Lugano valley and Switzerland, means that the town has always been an important trading centre. As always, trade brings traffic, but away from this the town is well worth the visit. During the Ten Years War, Menaggio chose the wrong side and was destroyed. It was a mistake the townsfolk made again several times in medieval times; they also picked fights with the Spanish and the Austrians during their periods of dominance. Success at trading had clearly fostered an independence of mind. The town has a very good beach – something of a rarity on Lake Como – and one of the most romantically sited golf courses in Italy. It is also a good centre for exploring both the Val Menaggio – the road to Porlezza and Lake Lugano – and the hills to the northwest. The Val Menaggio road passes the little lake of Piano, once part of Lake Lugano but separated from it by a landslide. The lake is now the centre of a nature reserve.

From Menaggio the minor road to Pièsio and Breglia passes through Loveno, a village that is almost unchanged since early medieval times. From Breglia, a good walk climbs Monte Grona, yielding views of both Lake Como and Lake Lugano, while a longer walk follows the upper reaches of Valle Sanagra to reach Monte Bregagno and an even wider panorama.

Below: *The jagged rock towers of Monte Granna above Menaggio*

✚ 36C4
🍴 Il Ristorante, Hotel Corona, Largo Cavour 3 (££) ☎ 0344 32133
🚌 Regular buses from Como and Porlezza
⛴ Regular lake steamers; car ferries from Varenna/Bellagio
♿ Few

➕ 36C4

✉ At the northern end of
Lake Como's eastern
shore

🍴 Albergo Ristorante
Belvedere (££), Via
Olgiasca 53, Colico
☎ 0341 940330

🚢 Regular lake steamers
from Colico

Piona Abbey

☎ 0341 940331

🕐 Daily 8–7 or sunset

♿ Reasonable

🎫 Free

*The monks of Piona
abbey are famous for
their liqueurs and herbal
remedies*

PIONA ✪✪

At the northern end of Lake Como's eastern shore, two spits of land almost touch, creating the sheltered bay of Laghetto di Piona, the little Piona lake, beloved of sailors because of its gentle winds. At the point of the western headland sits the Abbey of Piona. It is likely that this site was an ancient and holy one even before the Christian era, and there was certainly a Christian church before the abbey was founded by the Cluniac monks in 1138. Early in the 20th century the abbey was taken over by Cistercians. The monks distil liqueurs and manufacture a variety of herbal remedies. One of the liqueurs, Gocce Imperiali, has a reputation for being really potent, while another, St Bernard's Elixir, sounds intriguing. Parts of the abbey are open to visitors. The church is the oldest section but the cloisters are the most interesting. Built in the mid-13th century, they are a lovely mix of Gothic and Renaissance styles. The campanile is an 18th-century copy of the original. Outside the abbey the small garden with its central fountain is a haven of peace, and there are wonderful views across the lake to Gravedona.

North of Lake Piona is Colico, built at the edge of the marshland of Piano di Spagna, famous for its wildlife and migrating birds. Close to the Valtellina, the valley of the Adda and the Spluga Pass, the town was by turns prosperous on trade and subject to attacks by bandits using the high passes to escape with their spoils. South of the abbey, Corenno Plinio is a pretty village named after Pliny the Elder, who loved this section of the lake. Just beyond is Dervio, filling a rounded headland where the lake is at its narrowest. The strategic importance of this is reflected in the sparse ruins of medieval fortifications built to aid control of shipping on the lake.

➕ 36C4

✉ On Lake Como's eastern
shore

🍴 Vecchia Varenna, Via
Scoscesa 10, (££)
☎ 0341 830793

🚌 Regular buses from
Lecco

VARENNA ✪✪

The houses of Varenna climb a steep hill on top of which sit the ruins of a castle (Castello Vezio) which was the last home of Theodolinda, a 7th-century Lombard queen. The castle controlled the lake at the point where it divides and, sat on its outcrop of the Grigna, was virtually impregnable. The castle gave the village which grew up around it a certain prosperity, which was enhanced when the survivors of Como's destruction of Isola Comacina made their homes here and opened a quarry for the black marble which forms outcrops near the town. The marble quarry

📷 Regular lake steamers
and car ferries

Villa Cipressi
☎ 0341 830113
🕐 Jun–Sep Mon–Fri
10–12:30, 3:30–6; Sat
and Sun 10–12, 4–7
👊 Cheap
♿ Reasonable

Villa Monastero
☎ 0341 830139/830179
🕐 Jun–Aug daily 9–12, 2–7;
Apr, Sep, Oct daily 9–12,
2–5
♿ Reasonable
👊 Moderate

Museo Civico Ornitologico
☎ 0341 830367
🕐 Jun to mid-Sep Mon–Fri
10–12, 3:30–6; Sat and
Sun 10–12; mid-Sep to
May Thu and Sat 3–5
♿ Reasonable
👊 Cheap

kept the town prosperous for many years. By contrast, the product of a later son of the town did nothing for the local economy. G B Pirelli was born in Varenna, but his tyre empire did not include a Varenna factory. The Pirelli calendars were never produced here either.

Besides the array of fine old houses, Varenna boasts two superb villas. **Villa Cipressi** in Via IV Novembre has terraced gardens going down to the lake edge and lovely views across the water. To the south of the town, **Villa Monastero** is even more impressive, both for its building and its grounds. The villa was constructed in 1208 for Cistercian nuns but in the 16th century the sisters acquired a reputation for conduct distinctly unchaste and the convent was closed on the orders of San Carlo Borromeo. The villa passed into private hands and was then acquired by the Italian government. It is now used as a summer school for the sciences. It is a beautiful building with a stone staircase rising from the lake, lovely arched windows and an arcaded terrace. The grounds are equally good, with fine shrubberies and masses of citrus trees.

Back in the village, birdwatchers will want to visit the **ornithological museum**, where all the species which have been seen on the lake are displayed.

> ### DID YOU KNOW?
> South of Varenna is Italy's shortest river, the 250m Fiumelatte (milk river), so called because its tumbling flow makes the water look like milk. The river is the 'overflow' of another stream, starting up only when melting snows raise the level in the permanent stream.

Above: *Famed for its villas, Varenna also has a beautiful old harbour*

VILLA CARLOTTA (► 26, TOP TEN)

Below: *Modern Bergamo seen from Città Alta*

✚ 37D3

Museo Donizettiano
- ✉ 9 Via Arena, Upper City
- ☎ 035 399269/219128
- 🕐 Tue–Sun 10–1, 2:30–5
- 🎟 Cheap

Accademia Carrara
- ✉ Piazza dell'Accademia 82A
- ☎ 035 399643
- 🕐 Tue–Sun 9:30–1, 2:30–6:45
- 🎟 Moderate, Sun free

Basilica of Santa Maria Maggiore
- ✉ Piazza del Duomo
- ☎ 035 223327/246855
- 🕐 Daily 9–12:30, 2–6:30 (4:30 from Nov–Feb)
- 🎟 Free

Colleoni Chapel
- ✉ Piazza del Duomo
- ☎ 035 4368403
- 🕐 Daily 9–12:30, 2–6:30 (4:30 from Nov–Feb; closed Mon)
- 🎟 Free

The Bergamo Valleys

The relatively unkown city of Bergamo has a long history and a beutifully preserved medieval heart. North of Bergamo two valleys, each with numerous branches, head back towards the mountains which form the southern ridge of the Valtellina.

BERGAMO ✪✪✪

Bergamo is two cities, the modern lower one and the medieval upper one (Città Alta). Though the main attractions are concentrated in the Città Alta, visitors should not be ignore the lower city. The monument to Bergamo-born Donizetti (► 14) is in Piazza Cavour, while the theatre named after him stands on the Sentierone, which links Piazza Cavour to Piazza Vittorio Veneto. The **composer's birthplace** and a **museum** to him can be visited in the upper city. The lower city also has two fine churches: San Bartolomeo, with frescoes by Lorenzo Lotto, and Sant'Alessandro in Colonna. The column outside the latter church, made from stone fragments, marks the reputed spot where the saint was martyred in 297. If you head up to the upper city by road rather than funivia, you will pass the **Accademia Carrara**, which has many fine paintings.

In the upper city, pride of place goes to Piazza Vecchia (► 20), but there is much else to see. In Piazza del Duomo stands the cathedral, dating from the mid-15th century (though the dome and façade are 19th-century). Beside the cathedral is the basilica of **Santa Maria Maggiore**, a 12th-century building with a superb porch in red and white marble and a sumptuous interior. Built into the side of the basilica is the **Colleoni Chapel**, built by Bartolomeo Colleoni, a *condottiere* (mercenary soldier) who twice captained Venetian forces against Milan and twice led the

Milanese against Venice, growing rich in the process. Colleoni constructed the chapel as his mausoleum: he died in 1476 just after the chapel was finished.

VAL BREMBANA ✪✪

Brembana is the westerly of the two valleys. The Brembo River's geography meant that until the 17th century only two difficult passes allowed entry into the valley, the isolation allowing the local folk to evolve a rich folklore, including their own dialect and architectural style. At Almenno San Bartolomeo, the **Museo del Falegname** is devoted to the local craft of woodworking. At Sedrina a picturesque series of bridges crosses the river. The rock here is limestone and has been eaten away by rain and river water to form caves. One, the **Grotte delle Meraviglie**, can be visited. Further on there is a good **museum of the valley** in Zogno. San Pellegrino Terme is the best known village in the valley. Once one of the leading spas in Lombardy, it is now famous for its mineral water, which can be found in almost every town in Italy. Beyond San Pellegrino there are enough small villages and remote side valleys to keep the visitor entertained for several days. At the head of the valley, Foppolo is the best developed ski resort in the area.

DID YOU KNOW?

High in Val Brembana is the village of Cornello dei Tasso, named after a local family who, in the 13th century, started one of Europe's first postal services. Later, they were licenced to hire out private vehicles called 'taxis', and the family name became that of the official Soviet news agency – Tass.

VAL SERIANA ✪✪

The lower reaches of the Serio river valley are industrialised, but the upper valley remains unspoilt. Abbazia is named after its 12th-century Cistercian abbey, a delightful building. Further on is Gandino with a medieval gateway and a fine 15th-century basilica with a baroque interior. From the village a chairlift takes visitors to a plateau that is a ski resort in winter and offers good walking in summer. On again is Vertova, where the church is surrounded by an arcade so that it looks like a hen protecting her chicks. An even more impressive church is found at Clusone. The Oratorio dei Disciplini has frescoes that include a 'Dance of Death', people and skeletons hand in hand. The final village in the valley is Valbondione, from where a walk reaches the Cascata del Serio, reputedly Europe's highest waterfall at 315m. Sadly the stream which feeds it is now diverted into a hydroelectric station, the waterfall only being 'turned on' during certain summer weekends.

🞧 37D3

Museo del Falegname

✉ Via Papa Giovanni XXIII, Almenno San Bartolomeo

☎ 035 549198/540035

🕐 Sat 3–6, Sun 9:30–12, 3–6

🍴 Palanca (£), Via Dogana 15 ☎ 035 640800

♿ Few

🍽 Cheap

Grotte delle Meraviglie

✉ Sedrina

☎ 035 251233

🕐 Closed for renovation

🍴 There are opportunities locally, but those travelling on to San Pellegrino Terme should try Tirolese (£), Via De Medici 3 ☎ 0345 22267

♿ None

🍽 Cheap

Museo della Valle

✉ Zogno

☎ 0345 91473

🕐 Tue–Sun 9–12, 2–5

♿ Few

🍽 Cheap

🞧 37D3

Eastern Lakes

Well removed from the collection of lakes in the west of Lombardy and Piedmont lie two further large lakes and a number of smaller ones. The way that these eastern lakes came into existence was, of course, similar – though there is a subtle difference which we will explore when reaching Lake Garda. There is, however, a slight change in climate, the lakes lying further from the mountains, and, particularly on Lake Garda, there are more beaches. As a result, both Iseo and Garda have become centres for sun-seeking holidaymakers. This does not mean that there is any shortage of interesting historical sites, beautiful villas and gardens, or walks to be enjoyed on high ridges. There are wonderful towns to visit – Brescia, with its Roman remains, Romeo and Juliet's Verona and the incomparable Venice. But there are also more centres geared mainly towards entertainment and pleasure.

> *' Sweet Sirmio, thou, the very eye*
> *Of all peninsulas and isles*
> *That in our lakes of silver lie*
> *Or sleep enwreathed by Neptune's*
> *smiles. '*

CATULLUS
(*c*84 BC–*c*54 BC)

———————————— ● ————————————

Malcesine, one of the highlights of Lake Garda

Lake Iseo

Lake Iseo is the fifth largest of the lakes, 24km long and 5km across at its widest. However, at that widest point the lake is almost filled by Monte Isola, the largest island not only on any of the lakes but on any lake in Europe. At its deepest point Iseo is 250m deep.

This lake has something for everyone. On its eastern shore is scenery as dramatic as that of Lake Como's northern reaches, and close to its western shore is a scenic curio of compelling presence. There are fascinating villages and, near the village of Iseo, the Sebino peat bogs of the Torbiere nature reserve are a big attraction for wildlife (especially bird) enthusiasts. Also at the southern end of the lake, and close to Iseo, there are good beaches – one served by one of the lake area's largest campsites.

Right: The erosion pillars of Zone are among the best examples in Europe
Below: Looking across southern Lake Iseo from Iseo harbour

What to See around Lake Iseo

ISEO ✪✪

Iseo has a 12th-century church which holds the remains of several members of the Oldofredi family, local lords in medieval times. One tomb is built into the façade. The Oldofredi were also responsible for the castle that is now incorporated into the village hall. The village's lake front offers walks with fine views.

Iseo can be used as a centre for exploring the southern part of the lake. To the west is Sarnico, terminus for the lake steamers. It is an interesting town with the remains of old fortifications, echoes of its past as a fishing port and buildings designed by Sommarciga, one of Italy's foremost Art Nouveau architects. Between Iseo and Sarnico is Paratico, which has a ruined castle, where it's claimed Dante once stayed. Northeastwards along the lake from Iseo, the village of Pilzone is pleasantly set behind a headland that is now dotted with hotels and campsites.

➕ 37D2
✉ Southern shore of Lake Iseo
🍴 Il Paiolo, Piazza Mazzini, 9 (££) 030 9821074
🚌 Regular buses from Brescia
🚢 Regular lake steamers
♿ Reasonable

LAKE ISEO'S EASTERN SHORE

The eastern lake shore is dominated by Monte Isola, a traffic-free island which offers excellent walking. The island is reached from Sulzano, from which a long uphill walk leads to the lovely 15th-century church of Santa Maria del Giogo. The next village is Sala Marasino, where the garden of Villa Martinengo includes the remains of a Roman villa among the flower beds. Then take the winding road towards Zone and Europe's finest examples of **erosion pillars** – tall towers of glacial moraine created by uneven erosion. Some of the pillars are spectacularly high and some, in a surreal touch, are topped by huge boulders that originally lay on the moraine's surface. On the eastern shore, the final village is Pisogne, where the church, Santa Maria della Neve, has been called the 'Poor Man's Sistine Chapel' for the quality of the frescoes by Romanino.

LAKE ISEO'S WESTERN SHORE

Before exploring the western shore it is worth taking a detour from Pisogne to visit the historically important Val Camonica. On the rocks of the valley prehistoric man has engraved and painted a **tribal record** which extends from at least 5,000 BC until the time of the Romans. The best of the work is in the vicinity of Capo di Ponte, where there is a museum on the engravings, and waymarked walks around the sites.

On the shore, Lóvere is the lake's main tourist resort, but is also a town of great character and interest. There are the remains of medieval fortifications, including three surviving towers, and an art gallery housed in the beautiful 19th-century Palazzo Tadini. Beyond Lóvere are further geological marvels, the two bögns of Castro and Zorzino. The bögns are huge sheets of limestone that plunge steeply into the lake.

 37E3

Erosion Pillars

 Zone – along a narrow, twisting road from Marone

 37D3

Parco della Incisioni Rupestiri (National Rock Engravings Park)

Capo di Ponte

Park: Tue–Sun 8–7:30 (4:30 from Oct–Feb) 0364 42140; Study Centre/Museum: Mon–Fri 8–4 0364 42091

 Albergo Tre Stelle, Via Zanardelli 11, Pisogne (££) 0364 87835

Regular bus service from Pisogne

Reasonable

Moderate

Food & Drink

The lakes area serves a typically Italian menu, though there are a few specialities in the mountains. As everywhere in Italy, the meal will consist of generous helpings and be served with a smile. In addition, the restaurant is likely to have a terrace overlooking the water. As a result, there will be three delights to every meal – the food, the service and the setting.

Definitely not Wienerschnitzel
One of the standards on most local menus is *Cotoletta alla Milanese*, breaded veal cutlets. In view of the former Austrian domination of the area, visitors are advised not to refer to this course as Wienerschnitzel even if the observation is accurate enough.

Many of the region's dishes are, of course, pasta based

Ristorante, Trattoria or Pizzeria?

Of these, the pizzeria is the cheapest and quickest eating house. The menu usually consists of pizzas only, although some also serve a limited range of pasta dishes and may even have a grill. Trattorias serves a more extensive menu, but the meals will be straightforward, with minimum frills. The *ristorante* can vary from somewhere serving a limited range of meals, but of the highest quality – a fish restaurant for example – to one serving a very wide range. By 'quality' here is not meant the quality of the actual food but of the menu. The majority of Italian restaurants serve excellent meals from kitchens of the highest standard. But here, as everywhere, menus can vary from the simple to the very highest standard of international cuisine, with meals from the plain and simple to the elaborate and palate-shattering.

Food

Pasta is a mainstay, of course, but there is also a surprising amount of rice eaten. To the south of Milan, around Pavia, there are extensive rice fields – a fact which surprises many visitors – and rice dishes are a speciality. *Risotto alla Milanese*, a rice and saffron broth, is found all over the lakes area. Rice is also often served with fish. The lakes are home to many species of fish but which is best is, of course, a matter of opinion. Try the perch, which is exquisite, or lake trout. the other favourite. For something very different, try missoltini, sun-dried fish.

Meals can begin with small portions of pasta or rice, but minestrone soup is almost always on the menu. Made with fresh local vegetables it can be a meal on its own. Meat dishes tend to be veal or steak, though lamb (*agnello*) can also be found. The famed meat speciality is *osso bucco*, veal braised with white wine and onions.

Salami for sale in Orta San Giulio

Another even more popular, but less well-known speciality, is *polpette*, meatballs stuffed with parmesan and ricotta. Around Lake Orta the speciality is *asino* – donkey, usually stewed leg – while in the nearby Ossola valley they favour *viulin* – salted leg of goat. On the mountains around Lake Como, rabbit (*coniglio*) is still popular, while the Valtellina (the valley from north Como to Sondrio) produces *bresaola* – dried salt beef. Rabbit is also the favourite meat in Bergamo cooking, where it is usually preceded by local pastas such as ravioli with sage and butter. Many meat dishes will be served with *funghi*. Try the porcini, which have a distinctive, mellow flavour.

Vegetarians will be able to enjoy the minestrone, one of the highlights of Italian cooking, and pasta dishes such as vegetable lasagne and spinach panzerotti. There are also delicious vegetable dishes such as aubergines baked in cheese. Vegans will need to ensure that their chosen pasta is egg-free. There are several very good vegetarian restaurants in Milan.

Drink

Though not normally noted for its wines, northern Italy does have several very good labels which deserve attention. From Piedmont, around Novara, come Barolo and Barbaresco, both full-bodied reds, and Asti Spumante, the famous sparkling white. Lombardian wines tend to be white if they originate on the Plain and red if they come from the mountains. Of the former, try Moscato, of the latter Sassella and Grumello. Lake Garda is the most famous local wine-growing area. Here, try the full-bodied red Valpolicella, the lighter red Bardolino or the dry white Soave. The label will specify the wine's quality. DS (Denominazione Semplice) has no quality standard; DOC (Denominazione di Origine Controllata) wines meet defined standards and come from officially recognised areas; while DCG (Denominazione Controllata e Garanzia) are wines of the highest standard.

To Stand or Sit

In cafés and bars you usually pay for your drink first, presenting the payment slip with your order to the man behind the bar who makes the drink. In many cafés and bars a different price is charged for sitting with your coffee than for standing with it at the bar, the latter being the cheaper. Decide if you really do want to sit or whether a quick coffee, standing and talking, will suffice. If you go for the latter ask the cashier for your drink *al banco* (at the counter).

Panettone

The famed local dessert is panettone, a light, buttery cake, usually with sultanas and lemon rind. It reputedly acquired its name from its inventor, Toni, an apprentice pastry chef in Milan a century or so ago. When Toni's dough didn't rise, he added the butter and the sweet ingredients and served it as a new form of cake. The customers loved it and pan de Toni – Toni's cake – was born.

Brescia

Brescia is Lombardy's second city, with a population of about 200,000. It stands at the mouth of the Val Trompia, which descends from the pre-Alps of Lombardy's northern border. The city has some of Italy's best Roman remains as well as excellent medieval buildings.

COLLE CIDNEO

The oldest part of the city is the hilltop of Colle Cidneo, where there are Roman remains, the ruins of a 5th-century church and the 14th-century Visconti castle. In the castle is a Risorgimento museum and an arms museum.

Risorgimento Museum
- ✉ Colle Cidneo
- ☎ 030 44176
- 🕐 Jun–Sep Tue–Sun 10–5; Oct–May Tue–Sun 9:30–1, 2:30–5
- 🍴 La Sosta, Via San Martino della Battaglia 20 (£££) ☎ 030 295603
- ♿ Reasonable
- 🚻 Moderate

PIAZZA DUOMO

There are two cathedrals here, the older one (Duomo Vecchia or Rotonda) dating from the 11th century. It has a severe look, but an unusual circular design, and some remarkable treasures, including a sliver of the True Cross and a Holy Thorn. The newer cathedral is 16th-century baroque, but with a much newer dome. North of the cathedrals is the 13th-century Broletto and the Torre del Popolo, the people's tower.

Arms Museum
- ✉ Colle Cidneo
- ☎ 030 293292
- 🕐 Jun–Sep Tue–Sun 10–5; Oct–May Tue–Sun 9:30–1, 2:30–5
- ♿ Reasonable
- 🚻 Moderate

PIAZZA LOGGIA

The Loggia replaced the Broletto as the town hall after it was constructed in the 15th century and still maintains that function. The lower floor of the building was designed by Bramante, while the upper floor was by Palladio, a remarkable pedigree. Opposite the Loggia is the Palazzo dell'Orologio, topped by two Venetian figures in distinctly Moorish style. The picturesque older quarter of the city lies close to the piazza.

Above: *Colle Cidneo, which incorporates sections dating from Roman to medieval times*

VIA DEI MUSEI ✪✪✪

Brescia's real treasures lie in this street. Here stand the ruins of the **Capitoline Temple** and those of a 1st-century AD theatre, which itself stood at the edge of the forum. Further along the road is the **Museo della Città**, housed in the 16th-century monastery of San Giulio, though the site also has the remains of an 8th-century Benedictine nunnery and a 9th-century basilica. The complex houses collections, which, until very recently, formed the town's Roman and Christian museums. The Roman treasures include such treasures as a 1st-century bronze Winged Victory and six bronze busts of 2nd- and 3rd-century emperors. The Christian collection has many priceless items, the best of which include the Lipsanoteca, a 4th-century ivory reliquary and the 8th-century jewel-encrusted Cross of Desiderius.

✚ 37E2

Museo della Città
✉ Via dei Musei 81B
☎ 030 2977834
🕐 Jul–Sep Tue–Sun 10–8 (Wed, 10); Oct–Jun Tue–Sun 9:30–5:30
♿ Few
💵 Moderate

DID YOU KNOW?

Brescia's Capitoline Temple was built in AD 73 by the Emperor Vespasian. It was covered by a landslide centuries ago and only rediscovered in 1823. It is currently being restored.

VAL SABBIA AND LAKE IDRO ✪

East of Brescia, about halfway between the city and Lake Garda, the N45 road heads north, soon reaching the Chiese river. Geography prevents the Chiese from flowing into the lake, though it seems to want to, bypassing it by just 3km at Salò. From that point, near Tormini, the N237 follows the river closely as it flows through the Val Sabbia near a series of pretty villages. At Sabbio Chiese, the old castle on a large rock outcrop has been transformed into two churches, one on top of the other. Beyond Sabbio Chiese, the valley narrows, the church at Barghe seeming to grow out of the rock. Continue through Vestone, from where roads lead off into the mountains, to reach Lake Idro.

Idro is the highest lake in Lombardy, lying 368m above sea level, 11km long and up to 2km wide. In places, especially on the north-western shore, the surrounding mountains fall so steeply into the water that from the opposite shore they seem to rise vertically. Idro, the lake's largest village, lies just off the main road. It is a holiday village – here, and at nearby Crone and Vantone, the campsites fill rapidly in the summer. There are more campsites on the western shore, especially near Anfo, where there is a Venetian-built castle on the Rocca d'Anfo. Just beyond Anfo a road winds towards the mountains, reaching Bagolino, a very pretty village of narrow streets. Back on the shore road, the visitor reaches Ponte Caffaro, the last village of Val Sabbia.

✚ 37E3
🍴 Alpino, Crone, Via Lungolago 20, near Idro (££) ☎ 0365 83146
🚌 Regular buses from Brescia and Desenzano del Garda
♿ Few

Barghe in Val Sabbia

Lake Garda

Lake Garda differs from the other great lakes in that it thrusts out into the Lombardy Plain some distance beyond its retaining valley walls, an example of the power of large glaciers. Beyond the hard ridges that restrained the glacier to the north, the ice fanned out in textbook style, creating the wide sweep we now see. The glacier piled up many metres of moraine on the Plain, the lake being formed behind this morainic dam. So thick is the deposit of moraine that it accounts for 149m of the lake's maximum depth of 346m.

Garda is best known as a holiday lake, with a string of campsites along its eastern shore and many more on the shore line north of Desenzano. But it has other fine features too – the historical towns of Sirmione and Malcesine, good walking areas in Tignale, Tremosine and Monte Baldo, and excellent restaurants, serving food that is best enjoyed with a glass of local wine.

Monte Garda names both the town and the lake below it

The old harbour is one of the highlights of Desenzano

DESENZANO DEL GARDA ★★

Desenzano is the most important town on the southern lake, with a railway station on the Milan–Venice line and its own exit from the A4 *autostrada*. The site has been important for centuries, the Romans having built a fort here on the Capo la Terra, the highest part of the present town. In medieval times a castle was built on the remains of the Roman works. Roman Desenzano is also remembered at **Villa Romana**, the excavated remains of a 3rd- or 4th-century villa. The prize exhibit in what is considered the most important Roman villa in northern Italy is over 200sq. m of surviving mosaic, depicting hunting scenes and scenes of domestic and local life. There is a small museum where the best of the excavated finds are displayed. The town also has a **museum** exploring the pre-Roman history of the area. The 16th-century Duomo is also worth visiting to see *The Last Supper* of the Venetian painter Tiepolo, a very dramatic version. There are also works by other artists of the Venetian school.

Desenzano has a very picturesque old harbour, its edges dotted with trees and an array of fine buildings, some arcaded. A market is held close to and around the harbour on Tuesdays. This is one of the best local markets and a very good one at which to absorb the atmosphere of a small Italian town. At night the old harbour is a very romantic place for a quiet stroll. Equally good is a walk along the tree-lined lake front.

Close to Desenzano the village of Padenghe sul Garda is worth visiting. Houses here have been built within the walls of an old castle, giving it a medieval feel.

37E2

Bagatta alla Lepri, Via Bagatta 33, (££) ☎ 030 9142313

Regular buses from local towns and villages

Desenzano is the headquarters and terminus of the Garda lake steamers

Train station on line from Milan to Venice

Villa Romana

Via Crocefisso 22

Tue–Sun 8:30–7:30 (5 from Oct–Feb)

030 9143547

Moderate

Good

Museo Civico Archeologico

Via Anelli 22

Tue and Fri–Sun 3–7

030 9144529

Few

Moderate

37F2

Tobago, Via Bellini 1,
Garda (££) ☎ 045
7256340

Regular buses along the
eastern lake shore

Regular lake steamers

Reasonable

**Museo Castello
Scaligero (Tower
Museum)**

Torri del Benaco

Tue–Sun 9:30–12, 3–5

045 6296111

Regular buses along the
eastern lake shore

Above: *Vines at Bardolino
growing grapes for the
famous red wines of the
region*

GARDA ✪

The town named after the lake stands below Monte Garda, a natural fortress topped by the remnants of several castles, the last built by the Scaligeri. Under Scaligeri rule the town's Palazzo dei Capitano was also built, though the name derives from the time of Venetian rule, when the building housed the Serenissima's Captain of the Lake, the local official. A much more impressive building is the Villa Albertini, a romantic, castle-like villa where the treaty was signed which united Piedmont and Lombardy, which many historians date as the start of the Risorgimento. More local history is on display at the **museum of Torri del Benaco** (housed in the remains of yet another Scaligeri castle), the next village along the eastern shore. This museum also includes several examples of the prehistoric rock engravings found on Monte Luppia and at Punta San Vigilio, both close to Garda. The Punta itself should be visited – though surviving examples of the rock carvings are extremely difficult to find. It is one of the most beautiful places on the lake, with tremendous views across to Manerba and the Salò bay. At the tip is a dignified little church – it has a niche statue which is only visible from the water.

Torri del Benaco lies to the north of Garda – it is linked to Maderno by Lake Garda's only car ferry – while to the south is Bardolino, famous for its red wine which is produced from the vineyards that cover the hillside above the town.

LAZISE

Lazise has another of Garda's Scaligeri castles, almost as impressive as that at Sirmione, though not as well sited. The castle is now a private house and cannot be visited. In former times, a chain could be drawn from the castle across the harbour mouth and behind its protective 'wall'. When Lake Garda formed part of the Venetian Republic, a fleet of warships was maintained here, an amazing fact given the size of the harbour, which seems far too small to have fulfilled such a role. The Venetians referred to Lazise as the 'Key to Lake Garda' because the fleet controlled the southern lake. Today the warships are long gone, the harbour occupied only by a few fishing boats and pleasure craft. Around the harbour are a number of small hotels and cafés that are guaranteed to make any stay in the town a delight. As well as the castle, the town also has sections of the equally impressive arched medieval town wall complete with fishtail embattlements.

37F2
On the eastern shore of Lake Garda
Bastia, Via Bastia (££)
045 6470099

LIMONE SUL GARDA

It is assumed that the village was named after the lemon trees which, some believe, were grown here for the first time in Europe and made the early village prosperous. Others claim the lemon story is a legend and that the village is actually named after a son of the god Benacus. The lemon story is certainly supported by the bushes which now grow in profusion, as do orange and mandarin trees. A new road, the Gardesana Occidentale, now speeds visitors along Garda's western shore, bypassing Limone, which has, thankfully, become a quiet place again as a result. The discerning can stroll in peace, delighting in the houses of the old quarter with their balconies and flower boxes, and the village's setting below dazzling white cliffs. Amid such beauty, the inscription on the external wall of the church of San Pietro set in an olive grove on a hill close to the village comes as a shock. It tells of plague in 1630, a poor olive harvest in 1822 and the cruel winter of 1857, leading to an exodus from the village.

37F3
On the western shore of Lake Garda
Bellavista, Lungolago Marconi (£) 036 5954522
Regular buses along the western lake shore
Regular lake steamers
Reasonable

Above: *A children's playground in the shadow of the castle at Lazise*

85

37F3

Trattoria Vecchia
Malcesine, Via Pisort 6 (£)
☎ 045 7400469

Regular lake steamers

Regular buses along the
eastern lake shore

Castle/Museo Pariani

✉ On Lake Garda's eastern
shore

☎ 045 7400837

🕐 May–Sep daily 9–8;
Oct–Mar Sat and Sun
9–1, 3–6

♿ Reasonable

💰 Moderate

Palazzo dei Capitani

☎ 045 7400024/7400346

🕐 May–Sep daily 9–8

♿ Reasonable

💰 Moderate

MALCESINE

Some visitors would argue that Malcesine deserves a place in the 'Top Ten' of the Lakes area, and, after Sirmione, it is probably the most delightful of all Garda's villages. Certainly, the view of the castle from the beach and several picturesque parts of the old village make a trip to the town a must. The section of Garda's eastern shore which lies in Veneto is occasionally called the Riviera of Olives, and Malcesine is the area's undoubted capital. The castle, built in the 14th century, remains almost complete and now houses the **Museo Pariani**, a museum of the lake, with exhibits including information on the towing of war galleys to Torbole (➤ 88). There is a bust of Goethe in the castle courtyard.

Within the town any walk will be worthwhile. The **Palazzo dei Capitani**, the headquarters of the Venetian lake captains (officials), near the harbour is the most impressive building, but there are many other exquisite houses, some reached along narrow arcaded streets. On the north side of the village is the lower station of the funivia to Monte Baldo (➤ 12–13).

Malcesine's castle is one of the most striking on the lakes

PESCHIERA DEL GARDA ✪✪

Between Sirmione (► 23) and Peschiera the visitor crosses from Lombardy to Veneto, making Peschiera the first village of the Riviera of Olives. Because of its position, where the Mincio river leaves the lake, the site of Peschiera has always been important. The Romans had a town here, while under the Lombards a fishing village grew up, and the Scaligeri built a castle and a walled harbour to defend the river crossing. The castle is mentioned by Dante in the *Divine Comedy*. It was destroyed by the Austrians but they reinforced the walls, making the village one of the corners of their 'defensive quadrilateral'. After the Austrians were defeated the walls were not needed, but were too massive to demolish.

West of Peschiera, visitors can see the sites of the two battles of 24 June 1859. On that day, a Piemontian army under Vittorio Emanuele II fought the right wing of the Austrian army close to a village now called San Martino della Battaglia, while a short distance to the south, at Solferino, the French under Napoleon III attacked the main Austrian army under Emperor Franz Josef. Over 40,000 men were killed or wounded, the defeated Austrians being allowed to retreat by the exhausted victors. Today, each of the sites has a commemorative tower (though the one at San Martino predates the battle) and an ossuary chapel. The Solferino tower houses a museum of the battle.

✚ 37F2
✉ At the eastern end of Lake Garda's southern shore
🍴 Cristina Franco, Piazza Aleardi, 5, Peschiera del Garda (££) ☎ 045 7550931
🚌 Regular buses from Desenzano

Above: Though famous for its fortifications, Peschiera also has tranquil areas

DID YOU KNOW?

In June 1859, while the battle of Solferino was raging, a Swiss traveller, J Henri Dunant, was holidaying nearby. After the battle he visited the scene and was appalled by the suffering of the wounded, many of them dying in stifling heat from thirst and the lack of medical attention. Dunant wrote *Souvenir of Solferino*, an account of his visit, which was published in 1862. This led to the foundation of the International Red Cross, who erected a memorial on the centenary of the battle, built of stone from member nations all over the world.

Riva's climate and setting ensure that the pavement cafés are popular

---

🕂 37F3
✉ At the northern tip of Lake Garda
🍴 La Rocca, Piazza Cesare Battisti (££) ☎ 0464 552217
🚌 Regular buses along both lake shores
🛳 Regular lake steamers

Castle/museum
☎ 0464 573869
🕐 Tue–Sun 9:30–5:30
✋ Moderate
♿ Reasonable

🕂 37E2
✉ In a deep bay of Lake Garda's western shore
🍴 Villa Rimbalzello, Via Trento 28 (££) ☎ 0365 22782
🚌 Regular buses from Desenzano
🛳 Regular lake steamers

RIVA DEL GARDA ✪✪

Situated at the northern end of the lake, Riva is Garda's most famous holiday resort. The town handles this fame with grace, managing to maintain its character as a fishing/trading port even though the visitors outnumber the locals. The heart of the town is Piazza Tre Novembre, dominated by the Torre Apponale, a 13th-century clock-tower, and the arched buildings of the old town hall. Just a step away is the **moated castle** built to protect the town from pirates. The castle now houses a small museum of local history and an art gallery, and its irresistible approach – over a double-arched bridge and now fixed drawbridge – ensures a steady stream of visitors. Among other things, these visitors can see artefacts from the prehistoric dwellings discovered beside Lake Ledro, the tiny lake to the west of Riva. From the town, visitors can drive to the top of Monte Brione or take the funivia for the short ride to the Bastione for tremendous views of the lake.

SALÒ ✪✪

Salò is set at the furthest reach of an inlet of the Lake Garda, an enviable position which shelters it from winds. The town has a fine 15th-century cathedral which houses some excellent artwork including a polyptych by Paolo Veneziano. Look out for the equally attractive 16th-century Palazzo Municipale. On the first floor is a bust of Gasparo Bertolotti (known as Gasparo da Salò), who is usually credited with the invention of the violin.

North of Salò is Gardone Riviera. Here, be sure to visit the **Botanical Gardens,** first planted by Dr Arthur Hruska early in the 20th century and since taken over by the artist André Heller, who has added works combining art and ecology. Also worth visiting is **Il Vittoriale** (Vittoriale degli Italiani) an extraordinary complex constructed by Gabriele d'Annunzio, regarded as one of Italy's most flamboyant characters. He was a poet and soldier, and leader of the disastrous campaign to occupy Fiume (Rijeka) in 1919. In his will d'Annunzio left Il Vittoriale to the state. It is a whole collection of buildings, many in art nouveau style, and an open air theatre. D'Annunzio's old house is much as he left it – he disliked daylight and so painted most of the windows black – and visitors can also see his mausoleum, which is as extravagant as the man himself.

Beyond Gardone are the twin towns of Toscolano-Maderno, linked by Garda's only car ferry to Torri del Benaco, and Gargagno, where the Villa Fetrenelli was the seat of government of Mussolini's ill-fated Salò Republic.

SIRMIONE (➤ 22, TOP TEN)

TIGNALE/TREMOSINE (➤ 24, TOP TEN)

TORBOLE ✪

From a distance Torbole is a great sight: the fjord-like lake, the vast wedges of white rock falling into the water, and the colourful windsurfers who descend on the town each summer to exploit Garda's dependable winds dotting the lake. In Piazza Veneto, a plaque notes that Goethe set out from Torbole on the journey which ended with arrest at Malcesine, and it was here that Goethe began work on his *Iphigenia*.

Giardino Botanico

- ✉ Via Roma, Gardone Riviera
- ☎ 0336 410877
- 🕐 Mid-Mar to mid-Oct 9–6
- 🚌 Regular buses
- 🚢 Regular lake steamers
- 💶 Moderate

Il Vittoriale

- ✉ Gardone Sopra
- ☎ 0365 296511
- 🕐 Gardens: daily 8:30–8 (9–5 from Oct–Mar). House: Apr–Sep Tue–Sun 9:30–2; Oct–Mar Tue–Sun 9–1, 2–5. War Museum: Apr–Sep Tue–Sun 10–6
- 🚢 Regular lake steamers
- 💶 Moderate

- ✚ 37F3
- ✉ Northern tip of Lake Garda
- 🚌 Regular buses along both lake shores
- 🚢 Regular lake steamers

A row of elegant villas and hotels in Gargagno

Verona

Distance
5km

Time
2–4 hours, depending on museums visited

Start/End Point
In front of the Duomo in
Piazza del Duomo

Lunch
Olevo, 18 Piazza Brà (££)
☎ 045 8030598

The walk starts at Verona's Duomo. The cathedral was developed from an earlier, simpler church by heightening the façade and making other additions. The result, a fusion of Gothic and Romanesque, is not to everyone's taste. But as with the curate's egg, there are lovely parts – the 12th century doorway and, inside, Titian's *Assumption*.

Facing the Duomo, turn right and follow Via del Duomo out of the square, crossing two junctions to reach the church of Sant'Anastasia, Verona's largest church, on the left.

The church was begun in 1290 by Dominican friars. They laboured for 30 years but then building stopped for a century, and was not actually completed until 1423. The vast building is marvellously airy and has some interesting art. Look for the *gobbi* (hunchbacks) who support the holy water stoup, the frescoes and the figures in the Pelligrini Chapel.

Opposite the church, go along Corso Sant'Anastasia and turn second left (Via Fogge) to reach Piazza dei Signori.

The climb to the balcony is difficult but the queue to be serenaded or photographed there is long

In the centre of this magnificent square is a statue of Dante, his back to the Loggia del Consiglio, an elegant 15th-century Renaissance building. To Dante's left is the Palazzo degli Scaligeri, the palace of the city's medieval rulers. Beside the palace, an arch leads to the church of Santa Maria Antica and the **Tombs of the Scaligeri**, surrounded by a wrought-iron grille that incorporates the five-runged ladder symbol of the Scaligeri family. The greatest member of the Scaligeri was Francesco della Scala, who was known as Cangrande, Big Dog. Later members had similar nicknames, one actually being called Canrabbiaso, Mad Dog. Back in the square, facing Dante is the Palazzo dei Tribunali (law court). Beside this is the Palazzo del Comune (also called the Palazzo della Ragione), the old town hall, with its horizontal stripes of red and white marble. Its interior courtyard, the Mercate Vecchia (old market), is beautiful. The Comune is dominated by the **Torre Lamberti** which can be climbed for a terrific view of the Piazza dell'Erbe, reached through an archway. Piazza dell'Erbe is named after the herb market once held here. Today there is a more general market. Look out for the column topped by the Venetian lion.

Turn left in Piazza dell'Erbe to go along Via Cappello, soon reaching Casa di Giulietta (Juliet's House) to the left.

Shakespeare's story of Romeo and Juliet is based on one by the Italian writer Luigi da Porto, who in the 16th century retold a 12th-century legend of the feud between two Verona families, the Cappalletti and Montechi. Shakespeare 'anglicised' these names to Capulet and Montague. None of the sites in Verona which are claimed to be from the story have any basis in fact, but **Juliet's House** is probably the closest to the real thing. The house is about the right age, and the street is called Via Cappello (though this derives from an old inn, not from the ancient family name).

Either continue along Via Cappello, taking the next right and follow Via della Stella to Piazza Brà; or go back along Via Cappello for a few steps and turn left along Via Mazzini, Verona's busy shopping centre. To the left as you enter Piazza Brà is the Roman arena (► 25). Bear right along the Listone (► 25), then turn right along Via Roma to reach Corso Castelvecchio and the castle.

The castle was built by Cangrande II della Scala in the mid-14th century and subsequently used by all Verona's rulers. Ponte Scaligeri, which crosses the Adige river from the castle, was actually part of the original design, allowing defenders to be resupplied in the event of a siege. Today the castle houses the city's museum and art gallery.

Turn right along Via Castelvecchio, continuing along Corso Cavour and Corso Porta Borsari to rejoin the outward route at Sant'Anastasia. Now reverse your steps back to the Duomo.

Torre Lamberti offers an excellent view of Piazza dell'Erbe

Scaligeri Family Tombs
- Piazza dei Signori
- Visible only from beyond the grille, no entrance allowed
- Reasonable

Torre Lamberti
- Piazza dei Signori
- Mon 1:30–7:30, Tue–Sun 9–7:30
- None
- Moderate

Casa di Julietta (Juliet's House)
- 23 Via Cappello
- Mon 1:30–7:30, Tue–Sun 8:30–7:30
- Few
- Moderate

Castelvecchio (Castle/Museum)
- Corso Castelvecchio
- Tue–Sun 9–6:30
- Few
- Moderate

Venice

Few visitors to the lakes area will be able to resist the lure of Venice, one of the world's most fascinating cities. From many of the resort towns and villages – even from as far away as Lake Maggiore – day trips are available and these are good value because the independent traveller will find that parking is a problem. There is a huge car park at the edge of the Venetian lagoon, but it takes time to get into the city from there. Coach-borne visitors are usually dropped off and picked up in Piazzale Roma, close to both the Canal Grande and Rio Nuovo. By train, Venice is linked to Milan on a line which passes through Brescia, Desenzano del Garda and Verona. This offers a marvellous entry to the city as the station – where there is an information centre – stands beside the Grand Canal.

It is not possible to describe the main sites of Venice in a paragraph: whole books have occasionally failed to do justice to the city. It is built across over 100 islands and has 150 canals passing below 400 bridges, the waterways served by water buses, taxis and the famous gondoliers. On the Grand Canal, the visitor sees many of the main sites – this a trip from the train station to San Marco passing Ca d'Oro, its name deriving from the fact that it was once entirely gilded. Next, the visitor passes under the Rialto bridge, built in the 1580s and the most famous and elegant of all Venetian bridges. At the exit from the Grande Canal, to the right, is the impressive church of Santa Maria della Salute. Ahead, the boat will soon reach Piazza San Marco. Here are the real treasures of Venice – the Doge's Palace, the campanile (precisely rebuilt after the original collapsed in 1902), the Bridge of Sighs and the square itself.

Gondolas waiting for passengers on a Venetian canal

Where To...

Above: *A lakeside café on Lake Garda*
Right: *Not surprisingly, the lakes are famous for their fish*

Milan

Fast Food

Italy is a land of thousands of restaurants, the ones suggested here being a mere handful of those available. Here, as elsewhere, fast food outlets are increasing, though McDonalds and Burger King do not have it all their own way, the Autogrill chain offering competition that includes traditional pizzas and pasta.

4 Mori (££)

Just across from the entrance to the castle. In summer first class meals are served in the garden.
✉ **Largo Marie Callas, 1** ☎ **02 878483** 🕔 **Lunch, Dinner; closed all day Sat and Sun lunchtime** 🚇 **M1 Cairoli**

Al Girarrosto (££)

Traditional Tuscan cooking in elegant surroundings close to the Duomo.
✉ **Corso Venezia 31** ☎ **02 76000481** 🕔 **Lunch, Dinner. Closed weekend lunchtimes** 🚇 **M1 San Babila or Palestro**

Alfredo-Gran San Bernardo (£££)

Probably the best place in the city for true Milanese cooking. Try the risottos and the cotoletta Milanese. Not cheap, situated out by the Fiera (the international fair centre) but worth the journey and the bill.
✉ **Via Borgese 14** ☎ **02 3319000** 🕔 **Lunch, Dinner**

Al Mercanti (££)

Beautifully sited just a step away from the Duomo. Excellent menu and food and al fresco eating in a Renaissance market square. The connoisseur may not think it the finest place in town, but it is certainly the most romantic.
✉ **Piazza Mercanti 17** ☎ **02 8052198** 🕔 **Lunch, Dinner** 🚇 **M1 or M3 Duomo**

Antico Ristorante Boeucc (£££)

A superb restaurant tucked away in a quiet square just a short distance from the centre of the city. Excellent menu and cooking.
✉ **Piazza Belgioioso 2** ☎ **02**
76020224 🕔 **Lunch, Dinner; closed at luchtimes, Sat and Sun** 🚇 **M1or M3**

Bagutta (£)

Lovely little restaurant a bit off the beaten track, to the north of San Babila. Eat on the terrace and enjoy a place of great character as well as good food. Specialises in Tuscan dishes.
✉ **Via Bagutta 14** ☎ **02 76002767** 🕔 **Lunch, Dinner** 🚇 **M1 San Babila**

Biffi Scala (£££)

The other great eating house in central Milan. Highest quality cooking from a menu that combines local and international dishes .
✉ **Piazza della Scala** ☎ **02 866651** 🕔 **Lunch, Dinner; closed all day Sat and Sun lunchtime. Also closed early Jul** 🚇 **M1 or M3 Duomo**

Di Gennaro (£)

Very good pizza and pasta house, especially for those in a hurry as the service is speedy.
✉ **Via Santa Radegonda 14** ☎ **02 8053454** 🕔 **Lunch, Dinner; closed Thursdays** 🚇 **M1 Duomo**

Don Lisander (££–£££)

A great place to eat in summer when the tables are set in the beautiful garden. Good international menu which changes regularly.
✉ **Via Manzoni 12** ☎ **02 76020130** 🕔 **Lunch, Dinner; closed Sund** 🚇 **M1 or M3 Duomo**

Gazebo (£)

Charming little place with excellent cooking and service. Menu includes pizzas.

✉ Via Cadore 2 ☎ 02 59900029 🕐 Lunch, Dinner; closed weekends 🚇 M3 Porta Romana

Giannino (£££)
Typical Milanese cooking in a lovely setting. Delightful rooms and an exquisite garden for alfresco eating in summer.
✉ Via Sciesa 8 ☎ 02 55195582 🕐 Lunch, Dinner; closed Sun

Gocce di Mare (££)
Very elegant restaurant. Ideal for continuing the fish experience of the lakes as it has one of Milan's best fish menus.
✉ Via Petrarca ☎ 02 4692487 🕐 Lunch, Dinner; closed weekend lunchtimes 🚇 M1 Conciliazione

Il Giardino di Giada (££)
Something a little different: this is one of the best Chinese restaurants in the city, tucked away in the street behind the Palazzo Reale. Quality menu which always includes one 'budget' meal that is invariably good value.
✉ Via Palazzo Reale 5 ☎ 02 8053891 🕐 Lunch, Dinner 🚇 M1 or M3 Doumo

Joia (£££)
Considered to be one of the finest vegetarian restaurants in Italy.
✉ Via Castaldi 18 ☎ 02 29522124 🕐 Lunch, Dinner; closed Sat lunchtime and Sun 🚇 M3 Republica, M1 Porta Venezia

La Nôs (££)
Delightful place, elegant and usually with a piano player. One of the few Milanese restaurants with a car park. Excellent Lombard menu.
✉ Via Bramante 35 ☎ 02 3315363 🕐 Lunch, Dinner; closed Mon, and Tue lunchtime 🚇 M2 Moscova

Savini (££)
The most famous restaurant in the city, especially for the evening of the opening night of the La Scala opera season when the rich and famous, not only of Milan and Italy, but of Europe gather after the curtain has gone down. Menu and food as good as would be expected.
✉ Galleria Vittorio Emanuele ☎ 02 72003433 🕐 Lunch, Dinner 🚇 M1 or M3 Doumo

La Tavernetta-da-Elio (£)
A little out of the way, but quiet as a result and serving superb pasta dishes.
✉ Via Fatebenefratelli 30 ☎ 02 653441 🕐 Dinner; closed Sun and during the winter 🚇 M3 Turati

Trattoria all'Antica (£)
In the Naviglia district of the city, but well known for serving excellent food at reasonable prices and so justifiably popular.
✉ Via Montevideo 4 ☎ 02 58104860 🕐 Dinner; closed Sun and during winter 🚇 M2 San Agustino

L'Ulmet (£££)
A great, if expensive, place in winter when a welcoming fire burns away in the hearth. Superb menu and cooking and very pleasant surroundings.
✉ Via Disciplini, corner of Via Olmetto ☎ 02 606072 🕐 Lunch, Dinner; closed Sun and Mon lunchtime 🚇 M3 Missori

Pane e Coperto
The price you pay in your chosen restaurant will include *pane e coperto* – bread and cover – the cover being the charge for the table. In theory the bread charge allows the diner an unlimited supply of bread and/or bread sticks, though in practice it can be difficult to get the bread basket filled for a third time unless you are spending a lot of money.

Western Lakes

When to Drink Cappuccino

Italians drink cappuccino (known in the vernacular as cappuccio), the familiar coffee with frothed milk and, occasionally, a sprinkling of chocolate powder, first thing in the morning. Ask for a cappuccino at other times of day and you identify yourself as a tourist immediately.

Lake Orta

Sacro Monte (££)

Worth a visit for the setting and the house speciality desserts alone. Beautiful building, beautifully positioned. Limited seating, so booking is a good idea.

✉ **Via Sacro Monte 5, Orta San Giulio** ☎ **0322 90220** 🕐 **Lunch, Dinner**

Taverna Antico Agnello (£)

Delightful building in the old town. Excellent menu of local specialities.

✉ **Via Olivia 18, Orta San Giulio** ☎ **0322 90259** 🕐 **Lunch, Dinner**

Trattoria Toscana (£)

Surprisingly inexpensive, considering it's one of the best places on the lake. Specialises in lake fish dishes, but good overall menu.

✉ **Via Mazzini 153, Omegna** ☎ **0323 62460** 🕐 **Lunch, Dinner; closed Wed**

Villa Crespi (£££)

The smartest place on the lake. A lovely 19th-century villa set in parkland and with a reputation as *the* choice for local gourmets. The villa is also a small hotel.

✉ **Via Fava 8–10 (about 2km to the east of Orta San Giulio)** ☎ **0323 911902** 🕐 **Lunch, Dinner; closed most Weds and in winter**

Lake Maggiore

Al Camino (£)

Small – booking is advisable – but very nice, with good views of the lake and mountains, and a simple, but excellent, menu.

✉ **Via Per Comnago 30, on the road between Lesa and Comnago** ☎ **0323 7471** 🕐 **Lunch, Dinner**

Al Ponte (£)

Well-sited for those exploring the town or the northwestern shore. Very pleasant little restaurant with good food.

✉ **Via Roma 19, Cannero Riviera** ☎ **0323 788027** 🕐 **Lunch, Dinner**

Cá Bianca (£)

Eat good food from a simple menu while gazing out over the Malpaga castles.

✉ **Via Casali Cá Blanca 1, Cannero Riviera** ☎ **0323 788038** 🕐 **Lunch, Dinner**

Camin Hotel (£££)

Beautifully decorated restaurant in a very pleasant hotel. Excellent menu, chiefly of local specialities.

✉ **Viale Dante 35, Luino** ☎ **0332 530118** 🕐 **Dinner**

Charleston (£££)

Exquisite dining in one of Stresa's major hotels. International cuisine of the highest standard.

✉ **Hotel Regina Palace, Corso Umberti I 133. Stresa** ☎ **0323 31160** 🕐 **Lunch, Dinner**

Concordia (£)

Popular with the locals, which is usually a good sign.

✉ **Piazza Marchetti, Laveno** ☎ **0332 667380** 🕐 **Lunch, Dinner**

Dell Gallo (££)

Interesting place in Feriolo village where the road for the Simplon Pass splits from the lake road. Good menu, cooking and service.

✉ **Strasse Nationale Sempione 16, Feriolo** ☎ **032 328110** 🕐 **Lunch, Dinner**

Elvezia (££)

The best place on Isola Bella.

Good menu and cooking, and all in a romantic setting.

✉ **Isola Bella** ☎ **0323 30043** 🕐 **Lunch, Dinner**

L'Emiliano (£££)

Excellent menu and food in a lovely setting. The specialities are ravioli and lamb from the pre-Alps.

✉ **Corso Italia 50, Stresa** ☎ **0323 31396** 🕐 **Lunch, Dinner**

Ill Gabbiano (£)

Neat, inexpensive and with a surprisingly extensive menu.

✉ **Via Maggio 19, Baveno** ☎ **0323 924496** 🕐 **Lunch, Dinner**

Grotto Sant' Anna (££)

A little way out of the town, but worth the trip for the terrific surroundings. Very good local dishes.

✉ **Near the *orrido*, north of Canobbio** ☎ **0323 70682** 🕐 **Lunch, Dinner**

Isolino (£)

The wait for the car ferry from Intra to Laveno is never long. But just in case you have time to spare, this delightful little restaurant provides good cooking at a moderate price.

✉ **Piazza San Vittore 3A, Intra** ☎ **0323 53897** 🕐 **Lunch, Dinner**

Pace (££)

Another of Lake Maggiore's restaurants with a fine view of both lake and mountains. Well sited in charming Pallanza village, it's handy for Villa Taranto and also has a small number of rooms. Very good menu and excellent food.

✉ **Via Cietti, Pallanza** ☎ **0323 557207** 🕐 **Lunch, Dinner**

Piemontese (££)

Offers genuine Piedmontian cuisine in a very pleasant building.

✉ **Via Mazzini 25, Stresa** ☎ **0323 31396** 🕐 **Lunch, Dinner; closed Mon and, off-season, Sun**

La Piratera (££)

A must for those exploring the island and also for incurable romantics. Delightful setting and good cooking.

✉ **Isola Madre** ☎ **032 331171** 🕐 **Lunch, Dinner**

Pizzeria La Griglia (£)

Excellent pizzas in pleasant little building.

✉ **Via Cave 4, Baveno** ☎ **0323 924878** 🕐 **Lunch, Dinner**

Il Porticciolo (££)

Close to the church of Santa Caterina del Sasso and with a lovely view across the lake from the terrace. Specialises in lake fish, but has a good selection of other dishes.

✉ **Via Fortino 40, on the lakeside road about 2km south of Laveno** ☎ **0332 667257** 🕐 **Lunch, Dinner**

Lo Scalo (£££)

One of the best – some might say *the* best – places on the northwestern shore. Superb choice and cooking served in a lakeside garden.

✉ **Piazza Vittorio Emanuele II 32, Cannobio** ☎ **0323 71480** 🕐 **Lunch, Dinner; usually closed Mon and lunchtime Wed**

Il Torchio (££)

Quite small, so you may need to book, but it is worth the effort to do so.

✉ **Via Manzoni 20, Pallanza** ☎ **0323 503352** 🕐 **Lunch, Dinner; closed Wed**

Liscio

From mid-morning Italians drink strong black coffee – *liscio* – which comes in small quantities and small cups. It is usually taken with several heaped spoonfuls of sugar, but with or without the sugar it is lethal in quantity. Apparently there is actually a stronger version called *ristretto*.

Night Steamers

For something completely different, look out for the night steamers which offer a meal as you cruise, combining good food with a fascinating view of the lake villages, many of which floodlight their churches or main buildings.

Unione (££)

Arguably the only really authentic place to eat fish. Lake fish caught fresh during last night's fishing, cooked to perfection and served in romantic surroundings.

✉ **Isola Pescatori** ☎ **0323 933798** ⏱ **Lunch, Dinner**

La Vecchia Angera (££)

Excellent traditional Italian menu in pleasant surroundings. Good tourist menu at a very reasonable price.

✉ **Via Borromeo 10, Angera** ☎ **0331 930224** ⏱ **Lunch, Dinner; closed Thu**

La Vecchia Pesa (££)

Delightful little restaurant at the heart of the town. Straightforward menu but all food is very well prepared and served. There's an alfresco option (on the pavement to watch the world go by) in summer.

✉ **Via XXV Aprile 48, Luino** ☎ **0332 532408** ⏱ **Lunch, Dinner**

Lake Lugano
L'Ancora (££)

Lovely little place at the heart of the equally attractive village of Porto Ceresio. Typical Italian *albergo*, with a small number of rooms, restaurant and pizzeria. Very good food.

✉ **Via Mazzini 3, Porto Ceresio** ☎ **0332 917240** ⏱ **Lunch, Dinner**

Da Candida (££)

Terrific place in every sense. Lovely old building, excellent menu, fine service, good food. Try the lamb or one of the more exotic choices.

✉ **Via Marco 4, Campione**

d'Italia ☎ **091 6497541** ⏱ **Lunch, Dinner**

Hotel du Lac (£)

As elegantly sited as the name implies. Small and very well-kept hotel/restaurant, Simple menu, but very good.

✉ **Viale Ungharia 19, Ponte Tresa** ☎ **0332 5503089/550463** ⏱ **Lunch, Dinner**

Varese
La Bussola (££)

Set at the entrance to Valcuvia, and one of the best places for some distance.

✉ **Via Marconi 28, Cittiglio** ☎ **0332 602291** ⏱ **Lunch, Dinner**

Casa Radice (£££)

To the south of Varese, close to the A8 *autostrada*, and very handily placed for Malpensa Airport, if visitors are looking for a place to eat before departing. Very good menu and cooking.

✉ **Via Roma 8, Busto Arsizio** ☎ **0331 620454** ⏱ **Lunch, Dinner**

Colonne (££)

Worth visiting for the view, which is one of the best on the the western side of the lakes. The food is good too.

✉ **Via Fincarà, Santa Maria del Mote** ☎ **0332 224633** ⏱ **Lunch, Dinner; closed Wed and early Jun**

Lago Maggiore (£££)

The best place in town. The pistachio tortellini and the lamb with herb sauce are worth a journey of several kilometres.

✉ **Via Carrobbio 19, Varese** ☎ **0332 231183** ⏱ **Lunch (not Mon and Sun), Dinner**

Lake Como/ Bergamo

Como

Le Colonne (£)
Inexpensive but really good. Thoroughly recommended.
✉ **Piazza Mazzini** ☎ **031 266166** 🕐 **Dinner**

Da Pietro (££)
Nicely positioned in the cathedral square. Good cooking and pleasant atmosphere.
✉ **Piazza Duomo 16** ☎ **031 264005** 🕐 **Dinner**

Don Lisander (££)
Basement restaurant/pizzeria on the lake front road. Good choice and character.
✉ **Lungo Lario Trento 19** ☎ **031 261417** 🕐 **Dinner**

Hosterietta (££)
In the now-pedestrianised square a little way from Piazza Cavour. Traditional menu and excellent service.
✉ **Piazza Volta 57** ☎ **031 241516** 🕐 **Dinner; closed Mon**

Imbarcadero (£££)
Part of the Hotel Metropole Suisse in the main square. Superb menu and cooking and the option of eating on the square with lake views. Try the lake perch with rice.
✉ **Piazza Cavour 20** ☎ **031 277341** 🕐 **Lunch, Dinner**

Il Solito Posto (££–£££)
In the centre of the old town, with a garden for summer dining. Very good menu.
✉ **Via Lambertenghi 9** ☎ **031 271352** 🕐 **Dinner**

Lake Como

Anticho Ristorante Grotto dei Misto (££)
Situated in a sports complex. Specialises in lake fish dishes served on a terrace overlooking the water.

✉ **Pognana Lario** ☎ **031 309857** 🕐 **Lunch, Dinner**

Barchetta (£)
Neat little place at the heart of the town. Surprisingly extensive menu and very good cooking.
✉ **Piazza Roma 2, Argegno** ☎ **031 821105** 🕐 **Lunch, Dinner**

Bilacus (££)
Away from the lake front and up a steep side street. Very pleasant rooftop terrace and beautifully prepared and presented food.
✉ **32 Via Serbelloni 32, Bellagio** ☎ **031 950480** 🕐 **Lunch, Dinner**

Cermenati (££)
Very pleasant restaurant, well-sited for a tour of the town.
✉ **Corso Matteotti 71, Lecco** ☎ **0341 283017** 🕐 **Lunch, Dinner**

La Darsena (££)
One of the best places on this stretch of the lake. Good atmosphere and excellent food.
✉ **Via Alberto 8, Bellano** ☎ **0341 810317** 🕐 **Lunch, Dinner**

La Figurida (£)
Delightful little place serving a menu which includes local specialities.
✉ **Rogaro Ovest, near Cadenabbia** ☎ **0344 40676** 🕐 **Lunch, Dinner**

La Griglia (£)
Inexpensive and very good. Well-sited and with an alfresco option.
✉ **On the road from Argegno to Schignano/Intelvi** ☎ **031 821147** 🕐 **Lunch, Dinner; closed Tue**

Speciality Pasta
For local specialities in the pasta range, try pizzocheri – a Como/Valtellina speciality – which is a very rich black pasta served with melted butter; or gnocchi – pasta dumplings made with chestnut flour.

Funghi

The Italians eat many different sorts of *funghi* (mushrooms), but the most distinctively flavoured (and the most expensive) are porcini, which are excellent with meat and pasta dishes.

Harry's Bar (£)

Don't be put off by the name, this is one of the best places to eat in town. Nicely positioned – alfresco with lake views in summer.

✉ **Piazza Risorgimento 2, Cernobbio** ☎ **031 512647** ④ **Lunch, Dinner**

Imperialino (£££)

Very high quality restaurant, now bypassed by main lake road. As a result, peace and quiet is also on the menu.

✉ **Via Antica Regina 26, Moltrasio** ☎ **031 346600** ④ **Lunch, Dinner**

La Laconda dell'Isola (££)

Romantically sited on Lake Como's island – one of the few buildings on the now-deserted island. Limited menu, but well cooked and served with style.

✉ **Isola Comacina** ☎ **0344 56755** ④ **Lunch, Dinner**

La Lanterna (££)

Very good trattoria which also styles itself as a 'steakhouse'. Good choice for carnivores.

✉ **Corso Promessi Sposi 14, Lecco** ☎ **0341 355066** ④ **Lunch, Dinner**

Ricciolo (££)

Beautifully positioned and very quiet, as the main road bypasses the village.

✉ **Olcio, a small village to the north of Mandello del Lario** ☎ **0341 732546** ④ **Lunch, Dinner; closed Sun evenings and Mon**

Touring (£)

Wonderful views of Lake Lugano and the Alps. Limited menu, but excellent food.

✉ **Via Vetta Sighignola 40, Lanzo d'Intelvi** ☎ **031 840688/ 840692** ④ **Lunch, Dinner**

Trattoria del Vapore (££)

Very pleasant restaurant with excellent food.

✉ **Via Garibaldi 17, Cernobbio** ☎ **031 510308** ④ **Lunch, Dinner**

Vecchia Varenna (££)

One of the best places to eat on the northern end of Lake Como's eastern shore.

✉ **Via Scoscesa 10, Varenna** ☎ **0341 830793** ④ **Lunch, Dinner**

Bergamo & the Bergamo Valleys

Colleoni & dell'Angelo (£££)

Absolutely superb, with a terrific menu of Bergamo dishes, good cooking and excellent service in a magnificent palazzo.

✉ **Piazza Vecchia 7, Bergamo Upper City** ☎ **035 232596** ④ **Lunch, Dinner**

Da Vittorio (£££)

Famous across the region as a restaurant for gourmets. Speciality pasta dishes.

✉ **Viale Papa Giovanni XXIII 21, Bergamo** ☎ **035 213266** ④ **Lunch, Dinner**

Taverna Valtellinese (££)

Situated in the Bergamo's lower city. Serves a range of typical dishes from the Valtellina.

✉ **Via Tiraboschi 57, Bergamo** ☎ **035 243331** ④ **Lunch, Dinner; closed Mon**

Tirolese (£)

Claiming to cook authentic Lombardian food. Good menu and cooking, and nicely positioned.

✉ **Via De Medici 3, San Pellegrino Terme** ☎ **0345 22267** ④ **Lunch, Dinner**

Eastern Lakes

Lake Iseo

Al Desco (££)
Superb fish restaurant – but with good pasta dishes too – in a lovely setting. Excellent value.
✉ **Piazza XX Septembre 19, Sarnico** ☎ **035 910740** 🕐 **Lunch, Dinner**

Il Paiolo (££)
The best on this section of the lake. Wide choice, with something for everyone. Very good desserts.
✉ **Piazza Mazzini 9, Iseo** ☎ **030 9821074** 🕐 **Lunch, Dinner; closed Wed**

Il Volto (£)
A surprising place – a menu which would do justice to restaurants charging twice the price.
✉ **Via Mirolte 33, Iseo** ☎ **030 981462** 🕐 **Lunch, Dinner; closed lunchtime Wed and Thu**

Brescia

La Sosta (£££)
Housed in a beautiful, elegantly decorated 17th-century building which compliments the good menu and fine food.
✉ **Via San Martino della Battaglia 20** ☎ **030 295603** 🕐 **Lunch, Dinner**

Trattoria Briscola (£)
To the north of the centre. A little way out, but diners can enjoy a view of the city.
✉ **Via Costalungo 18** ☎ **030 395232** 🕐 **Lunch, Dinner**

Lake Garda

Alla Scoglio (££)
This restaurant, with its garden and lake views, makes a detour worthwhile.
✉ **Via Barbacane 3, Bogliaco** ☎ **0365 71030** 🕐 **Lunch, Dinner**

Antica Trattoria alle Rose (££)
Delightful building and decor, good menu, fine food and service.
✉ **Via Costalungo 18, Salò** ☎ **0365 43220** 🕐 **Lunch, Dinner**

Bastia (££)
Excellent restaurant in a very pretty position.
✉ **Via Bastia, Lasize** ☎ **045 6470099** 🕐 **Lunch, Dinner**

Esplanade (£££)
Absolutely first class. Speciality pastas and such mouthwatering things as mountain lamb in herbs. Highly recommended.
✉ **Via Lario 10, Desenzano del Garda** ☎ **030 9143361** 🕐 **Lunch, Dinner**

Gallo Rosso (£)
Pleasant, excellent restaurant which does a special 'drink included' price.
✉ **Vicolo Tomacelli 4, Salò** ☎ **0365 520757** 🕐 **Lunch, Dinner; closed Wed**

Il Giardino delle Esperidi (££)
Beautiful garden restaurant with menu and food to match.
✉ **Via Mameli 1, Bardolino** ☎ **045 6210477** 🕐 **Dinner**

Il Molino (£)
Excellent fish restaurant.
✉ **Piazza Matteotti 16, Desenzano del Garda** ☎ **030 9141340** 🕐 **Lunch, Dinner**

Pizzeria al Marconi (£)
Out of the way, but well worth the visit for the terrace above the lake and the food.
✉ **Padenghe sul Garda** ☎ **030 9912563** 🕐 **Lunch, Dinner**

Exchange Rates
If you can use Visa or Mastercard then it is probably worthwhile, as the rate of exchange the major card companies can command is usually better than the tourist rate and you also avoid the commission charge. If not, then use lire, because the few shops which will take sterling or dollars will be offering an exchange rate well below the rate you can expect in a bank.

The Winter Months

Many hotels in the lakes area close during the winter months when trade is slack. If you are planning to visit during that period, it is advisable to check beforehand as you may well find your chosen hotel closed, even if the summer brochure assures you it will be open.

La Rocca (££)

Fine terrace with memorable views to accompany alfresco meals.

✉ Piazza Cesare Battisti, Riva del Garda ☎ 0464 552217 🕓 Lunch, Dinner; closed Wed

Signori (£££)

Lovely setting – eat while gazing across Lake Garda. Very good menu and excellent service and food.

✉ Via Romagnoli 23, Sirmione ☎ 030 916017 🕓 Lunch, Dinner

Tavernetta Fucine di Leonesio Francesco (£)

Good menu and excellent cooking – the food tastes so much better because of the effort involved getting here.

✉ Via Fucine 11, Vesio (Tremosine) ☎ 0365 951151 🕓 Lunch, Dinner

La Terrazza (££)

In view of the name, it comes as no surprise that there is a terrace with expansive lake views. Interesting menu.

✉ Via Pasubio 15, Torbole ☎ 0464 506083 🕓 Lunch, Dinner; closed Tue

La Tortuga (£££)

One of the best places on Garda's western shore. Specialities include lake fish and a secret fettucine recipe. Well worth a try, but space is limited so dinner booking is advisable. Tables are usually available at lunchtime.

✉ Via XXIV Maggio 5, Gargnago ☎ 0365 71251 🕓 Lunch, Dinner

Trattoria Vecchia Malcesine (£)

Lovely little place, full of character. Quite small, so booking is worthwhile to avoid disappointment.

✉ Via Pisort 6, Malcesine ☎ 045 7400469 🕓 Lunch, Dinner

Vecchia Riva (£££)

Limited seating so booking is advised, but worth the effort to enjoy the menu and the excellent cooking.

✉ Via Bastione 3, Riva del Garda ☎ 0464 555061 🕓 Lunch, Dinner

Villa Fiordaliso (£££)

Beautiful old palazzo. Famous for its fish dishes (particularly the lake perch), risottos and desserts. One of the best gourmet restaurants in the area.

✉ Via Zanardelli 132, Gardone Riviera ☎ 0365 20158 🕓 Lunch, Dinner

Verona

Accademia (££)

Midway between the Arena and Scaligeri Tombs. Very good menu and cooking.

✉ Via Scala 10 ☎ 045 8006072 🕓 Lunch, Dinner; closed Sun Sep–Jun

Il Desco (£££+)

Just a few steps away from the Scaligeri Tombs is Verona's most exclusive restaurant. Be prepared to part with a lot of money (150,000lire +), but also to be pampered and well fed.

✉ Via Dietro San Sebastiano 7 ☎ 045 595358 🕓 Lunch, Dinner

No. 18 Piazza Bra (££)

Half-way along the Listone, with views of the whole square and the Arena. Good menu and food, and magical at night.

✉ 18 Piazza Bra 18 ☎ 045 8030598 🕓 Lunch, Dinner

Milan & the Western Lakes

Milan

Cavour (££)

Situated in a fashionable part of town, only a short distance from the centre. Unusually, it has a vegetarian restaurant.

 Via Fatebenefratelli 21, 20121 Milano ☎ **02 620001 F 02 6592263** 🕓 **Jun, Jul and Sep–Nov**

Grand Hotel Duomo (£££)

Luxurious hotel. Some of the rooms have a view of the cathedral. Excellent facilities and a fine restaurant.

✉ **Via San Raffaele 1, 20121 Milano** ☎ **02 8833 F 02 86462027**

Grand Hotel et de Milan (£££+)

Almost off the price scale, with all possible facilities. Situated next to La Scala, within a short walk of the Duomo. Two excellent restaurants.

✉ **Via Manzoni 29, 20121 Milano** ☎ **02 723141 F 02 86460861**

Manzoni (££)

Located just off Via Montenapoleone, so not too far to carry the shopping bags. Good facilities but no restaurant.

✉ **Via Santo Spirito,20, 20121 Milano** ☎ **02 76005700 F 02 784212** 🕓 **Jun, Jul and Sep–Nov**

Rovello (£)

Just off Via Dante, which links the castle to the Duomo. Very small but very pleasant, although there is no restaurant.

✉ **Via Rovello 18, 20121 Milano** ☎ **02 86464654 F 02 72023656**

Western Lakes
Lake Orta
L'Approdo (££)

Pettenasco is a small village beside the lake just north of Orta San Giulio. The hotel makes the most of its position with a fine garden offering lake and mountain views. Good facilities and excellent restaurant.

✉ **Corso Roma 80, 28028 Pettenasco** ☎ **0323 89345 F 0323 89338** 🕓 **Jun to mid-Feb**

San Rocco (££)

Very comfortable, with a garden/terrace stretching down to the lake. Excellent facilities including a good restaurant.

✉ **Via Gippini 11, 28016 Orta San Giulio** ☎ **0322 911977 F 0322 911964**

Santa Caterina (£)

Situated about 2km to the east of the town. Good facilities, but no restaurant.

✉ **Via Marconi 10, 28016 Orta San Giulio** ☎ **0322 915865 F 0322 90377** 🕓 **Mid-Mar to Oct**

Lake Maggiore
Beau Rivage (££)

Well-sited in one of the best villages on the western shore. Baveno also is a good tourist centre. The hotel has excellent facilities including a small garden. Good restaurant.

✉ **Viale della Vittoria 16, 28831 Baveno** ☎ **0323 924534 F 0323 925253**

Camin Hotel Luino (££)

Not to be confused with the Camin Hotel Comegna in the village of Colmegna. Very comfortable and has an excellent restaurant.

✉ **Viale Dante 35, 21016 Luino** ☎ **0332 530118 F 0332 537226**

Camping

Italy has good camp sites, but they are not evenly spread across the lakes' area. Lake Orta has none, Lake Maggiore has few, and those are mainly on the eastern shore. Lake Como has none, though there is one close to the Como exit of the autostrada. They are equally sparse on Lake Lugano. By contrast, the eastern lakes – Iseo and Garda – have many sites, especially on the eastern shore of Lake Garda.

103

Classification

The Italian hotel classification system is not as straightforward as it might appear. Occasionally a star is added if a hotel has a swimming pool or other facilities, or one may be lost if it does not have a pool. It is always worth checking the list of facilities. If this seems a little limited, but the classification is high, you can be assured of a really excellent room.

Conca Azzurra (£)

Situated in a village just north of Angera. Tidy little hotel with reasonable facilities and a restaurant.
✉ Via Alberto 53, 21020 Ranco ☎ 0331 976526 F 0331 976721 🕐 Mid-Feb to mid-Dec

Giardino (££)

Very pleasant and well-sited. Excellent facilities and a good restaurant.
✉ Corso della Repubblica 1, 28041 Arona ☎ 0322 45994 F 0322 249401

La Fontana (££)

A little way to the north of Stresa, set back from the lakeside road in pretty grounds, well shaded by trees. Reasonable facilities, but no restaurant.
✉ Via Sempione Nord 1, 28838 Stresa ☎ 0323 32707 F 0323 32708 🕐 Jan to mid-Nov

Grand Hotel Bristol (£££)

Not quite as splendid as its near neighbour, but almost. A superb hotel with excellent facilities and restaurant.
✉ Corso Umberto I 73/75, 28838 Stresa ☎ 0323 32601 F 0323 33622

Grand Hotel et Des Iles Borromées (£££+)

One of the great hotels of the lakes area. Everything you could ask for, and then some more. Gardens, views of the Borromean Islands, excellent restaurant etc.
✉ Corso Umberto I 67, 28838 Stresa ☎ 0323 938938 F 0323 32405

Majestic (£££)

One of the best hotels in the area and beautifully sited beside the lake. All facilities and a superb restaurant.
✉ Via Veneto 32, 28922 Pallanza ☎ 0323 504305 F 0323 556379

Miralago (£)

Unpretentious, but very good. Good range of facilities and a very pleasant restaurant.
✉ Via Dante, 28821 Cannero Riviera ☎ 0323 788282 F 0323 787075 🕐 Mar–Oct

Verbano (££)

Romantically sited on Pescatori island. Visitors have the island to themselves when the crowds go home, but have to make the crossing to the mainland when they wish to travel. Facilities include restaurant.
✉ Via Ugo Ara 2, 28049 Isola Pescatori ☎ 0323 30408 F 0323 33129

Lake Lugano
Albergo L'Ancora (£)

Lovely little hotel in beautiful village beside Lake Lugano. Very good restaurant.
✉ Via Mazzini 3, 21050 Porto Ceresio ☎ 0332 917240 F 0332 920245

Hotel du Lac (£)

Elegantly sited. Small and well-kept and with an excellent restaurant.
✉ Viale Ungheria 19, 21037 Ponte Tresa ☎ 0332 550308/550463

Varese
City Hotel (££)

For those looking for a city hotel within reach of the western lakes. Positioned near the centre of Varese and with good facilities. No restaurant but good places just a short walk away.
✉ Via Medaglie d'Oro 35, 21100 Varese ☎ 0332 281304 F 0332 232882

Delle Arti (££)

Ideal for those wanting a hotel away from the lake side. Close to Val Cuvia and Val Ganna. Excellent facilities and restaurant.
✉ Via Luinese 18, Cunardo ☎ 0332 715002 F 0332 715288

Lake Como

Alberi (£–££)

Well-sited hotel for exploring Lecco, the Grigna mountains and the Lecco arm of the lake. Good facilities. No restaurant but close to some very good ones.

✉ **Lungo Lario Isonzo,4, 23900 Lecco** ☎ **0341 350992 F 0341 350895**

Barchetta Excelsior (£££)

The best position in town, right at the edge of the main square and facing the lake. Comfortable modern decor and a very good restaurant.

✉ **Piazza Cavour 1, 22100 Como** ☎ **031 3221 F 031 302622**

Centrale (££)

Fine old building in the centre of town, just a few steps away from the lake steamer quay. Excellent restaurant, with an alfresco option in the garden in summer.

✉ **Via Regina 39, 22012 Cernobbio** ☎ **031 511411 F 031 341900**

Florence (££)

A neat little hotel in the heart of the town. Good facilities and an excellent restaurant with garden service.

✉ **Piazza Mazzini 46, 22021 Bellagio** ☎ **031 950342 F 031 951722** 🕐 **Apr–Oct**

Grand Hotel Tremezzo (£££)

Superb hotel, one of the oldest on the lake and built in grand style with gardens to match. Some rooms share balconies overlooking the lake. Excellent restaurant.

✉ **Via Regina 8, 22019 Tremezzo** ☎ **0344 42491 F 0344 40201** 🕐 **Mar–Nov**

Grand Hotel Victoria (£££)

Beautiful old building in delightful grounds. Very good restaurant with alfresco option.

✉ **Lungolago Castelli 7/11, 22017 Menaggio** ☎ **0344 32003 F 0344 32992**

Grand Hotel Villa d'Este (£££+)

With a claim to being the finest hotel on the lakes, and one of the very best in Italy, the building is almost a museum. All the visitor could dream of is available.

✉ **Via Regina 40, 22012 Cernobbio** ☎ **031 3481 F 031 348844**

Grand Hotel Villa Serbelloni (£££+)

Magnificent and magnificently sited villa, now world-class hotel with a superb restaurant.

✉ **Via Roma 1, 22021 Bellagio** ☎ **031 950216 F 031 951529** 🕐 **Easter–Oct**

Royal Victoria (££)

Close to the car ferry so very good for those planning to travel around the lake. Great facilities and fine restaurant.

✉ **Piazza San Giorgio 5, 23829 Varenna** ☎ **0341 815111 F 0341 830722**

Bergamo

Arli (££)

Close to the funivia for the upper city and the lower city's shopping centre. Good facilities. No restaurant, but near many excellent ones.

✉ **Largo Porta Nuovo 12, 24121 Bergamo (lower city)** ☎ **035 222014 F 035 239732**

Cappello d'Oro (£££)

Just a short walk from the lower station of the funivia to the upper town. Very well appointed with a good restaurant.

✉ **Viale Papa Giovanni XXIII 12, 24121 Bergamo (lower city)** ☎ **035 232503 F 035 242946**

Terme (££)

Well-sited for an exploration of the Bergamo valleys. Good restaurant, but this is only open in the summer.

✉ **Via Bartolomeo Villa 26, 24016 San Pellegrino Terme** ☎ **0345 21125 F 0345 23497**

Farm holidays

Agriturismo is popular in Italy, visitors renting a self-catering flat, house or part-house on a working farm. Usually the farmer will supply home-grown vegetables and may even allow freedom of the farm itself. For details contact:

Agriturismo

✉ **Corso Vittorio Emanuele 101, 00186 Roma** ☎ **06 6852342/6852337**

Eastern Lakes

Supermarkets and Chains

The best local supermarkets are Coin and Standa, the latter having not only food, but clothing, toiletries etc. For young fashions at an affordable price look for the Ciao-Ciao shops.

Brescia and Lake Iseo

Ambra (£)
Small, but well positioned. Simple decor and limited facilities, but comfortable and welcoming.
✉ Porto Bagriele Rosa 2, 25049 Iseo ☎ 030 980130 F 030 9821361

Master (£££)
Lovely old palazzo close to the castle. Very comfortable.
✉ Via Appollonio 72, 25100 Brescia ☎ 030 399037 🖳 030 3701331

Moderno (££)
Small, very pleasant hotel near the centre of town.
✉ Piazza 13 Martiri 21, 24065 Lóvere ☎ 035 960607 🖳 035 961451

Lake Garda

Benacus (££)
Medium-sized secluded hotel. Rooms with balconies.
✉ Via Monte Brione 18, 38066 Riva del Garda ☎ 0464 552737 🖳 0464 551030 🕙 Apr–Oct

Caravel (£££)
Complex of buildings around a swimming pool. Terrific views and good restaurant.
✉ Via Tamas 2, 25010 Limone sul Garda ☎ 0365 91011 🖳 0365 954239

Castello (££)
Right at the lakeside with a small beach. Good facilities.
✉ Via Paina 3, 37018 Malcesine ☎ 045 7400233 🖳 045 7400180 🕙 Apr–Oct

Grand Hotel Terme (£££)
Luxurious hotel set at the lake edge for strolls over the drawbridge. Many facilities.
✉ Viale Marconi 7, 25019 Sirmione ☎ 030 916261 F 030 916568 🕙 Apr–Oct

Nonna Ebe (£)
Small, inexpensive hotel with good terrace restaurant and reasonable facilities.
✉ Via Calsone 9, 25087 Salò ☎ 0365 43639/520785 F 0365 520866

Sirmione (££–£££)
Romantically positioned within the town. Good facilities and an excellent restaurant.
✉ Piazza Castello,19, 25019 Sirmione ☎ 030 916331 F 030 916558 🕙 Mar–Nov

Villa Capri (££)
Glorious position. The lakeside garden offers shady trees and sunloungers.
✉ Via Zanardelli 172, 25083 Gardone Riviera ☎ 0365 21537 F 0365 22720 🕙 Apr–Oct

Vittorio (££)
Best hotel in town for position, right at the edge of the old harbour. Very pleasant. No restaurant, but easy access to some of the best in town.
✉ Via Porto Vecchio 4, 25015 Desenzano del Garda ☎ 030 9912245/9912258 F 030 9912270 🕙 Mar–Nov

Verona

Accademia (££)
Right in the heart of the old town. Good facilities and a vegetarian restaurant.
✉ Via Scala 12, 37121 Verona ☎ 045 596222 F 045 8008440

Due Torri Baglioni (£££)
Arguably the best in town and within a few minutes of the Arena and Listone. Excellent facilities and restaurant.
✉ Piazza Sant'Anastasia 4, 37121 Verona ☎ 045 595044 F 045 8004130

Shopping in Northern Italy

The cities of northern Italy offer a great experience to the confirmed shopaholic. The diversity in wealth between the south and north of Italy is of great concern both to the inhabitants of the south and to everyone with an interest in their fellow human beings, but an inevitable by-product is that the standard of living in the north is as high as any place in Europe, and the shops reflect the fact that the average northern Italian has a high disposable income.

The artistic heritage of the Italians means that style and quality are demanded by a well-heeled clientele. For the very latest and best in fashion and lingerie this is the place to come. Add the world renown of Italian leather and it is easy to see why many visitors go home with more baggage than they arrived with.

The best shopping is to be found in the main towns. The villages of the lakes area tend only to serve the locals with necessities and visitors with maps and souvenirs. As a result, for the real shopping experience, head for Milan, Verona, Bergamo, Brescia and, to a lesser extent the big lake towns such as Como. The exceptions to the rule are the famous visitor towns – Sirmione, Bellagio – where the annual influx of visitors has allowed the growth of good local shops. The theory seems to be that if you can afford to stay in the hotels you can afford to patronise the shops – and who could deny that this is a theory that holds good elsewhere.

Milan

As might be expected for a city of a couple of million people, Milan has many shopping centres. The one the visitor will head for is to the east of the Duomo. Via Vittorio Emanuele II leads from Piazza Duomo to Piazza San Babila. There are shops and shopping arcades on both sides. Close to the north side of San Babila, Via Montenapoleone leads off, and side turnings from it (on the right, for instance Via Sant'Andrea) lead to Via della Spiga, the other main shopping street. From the Duomo to Via della Spiga is a walk of about 15 minutes.

For **fashion and fashion accessories** Armani has shops in Via Sant'Andrea (No 9 – ladies' and men's) and Via Durini (No 23, children's wear and No 24, young fashions). Calvin Klein (No 14) and Moschino (No 14 – men's) are also in Via Durini, while in Via Sant'Andrea you will find Chanel (No 10A), Gianfranco Ferré (No 15), Hermes (No 21), Missoni (corner of Via Bagutta), Moschino (No 12 – ladies') and Trussardi (No 5). Via Montenapoleone has Byblos (No 42), Cerruti (No 20), Dolce e Gabbana (No 2 for ladies and No 26 for men), Krizia (No 6 – men's and leather), Ungaro (No 77), Valentino (No 20 – men's) and Versace (No 2). Christian Lacroix, Ermenegildo Zogna and Yves St Laurent can be found in Via Verri.

For **leather goods** the most exclusive shops are Alviero Martini Prima Classe (Via Montenapoleone 26), Bottega Veneta (Via Della Spiga 5), Bruno Magli (Corso

Shop without Luggage

Those wanting to shop, or just window shop, in Milan can do so after dropping off their luggage in the left-luggage office at Linate Airport. Outside the airport's main entrance look for bus no 73. You buy your ticket at the machine beside the stop (coins only) or at the bar just inside the airport. No 73 runs every 10 minutes or so and terminates in Piazza San Babila just a few steps away from the main shopping centre.

Village Markets

Many of the towns and villages around the lakes have regular markets. For perishable goods – fruit, vegetables – these are held daily and it is worthwhile checking them out if you are self-catering or looking for healthy snacks.

Vittorio Emanuele II, corner of San Paolo), Louis Vuitton (Via Montenapoleone 14) and Mario Valentino (Via Montenapoleone 10).

Bottega Veneta and Bruno Magli are also excellent for **shoes**, as are Ferragamo Salvatore (Via Montenapoleone 3), Sergio Rossi (Via della Spiga 15), Teras (Via Torino, on the corner of Via Lupetta), Vergelio (Corso Vittorio Emanuele II 10) and Vierre (Via Montenapoleone 27).

The most exclusive **jewellery** can be found at Agalma (Via San Tommaso 8), Buccellati (Via Montenapoleone 4), Bulgari (Via della Spiga 6), Cartier (three shops, in Via Montenapoleone, Corso Vercelli and Via Omboni), Cusi, Damiani and Tiffany Faraone (all in Via Montenapoleone) and Scavia (Via della Spiga 9).

For luxurious **lingerie** try La Perla (Via Montenapoleone 1) or Prada in Via della Spiga.

As an antidote to all these expensive items, La Rinascente, the **department store** opposite the north side of the Duomo is well worth visiting. On nine floors, and with an exhibition floor above that, there is as good a choice as anyone could wish for.

Galleria Vittorio Emanuele II has many **bookshops**, but those looking for books in English should try:

American Bookshop
✉ Via Camperio 16 ☎ 02 878920

English Bookshop
✉ Via Aristo, on the corner of Via Mascheroni ☎ 02 4694468

Milan has numerous **markets**, there being one for every day of the week. The main tourist office, close to Piazza Duomo, will have the

details. A particularly interesting market is the flea market in Viale Gabriele D'Annunzio on Saturdays. There are also several antiques markets. Those in Ripa Ticines/Alzaia Naviglio Grande on the last Sunday of the month (but not July) and in Via Fiori Chiari on the third Sunday of the month are reckoned to be the best.

Bergamo

The best shopping in town is in the streets close to Piazza Matteotti/Piazza Vittorio Veneto – Il Sentierone and Via Torquato Tasso, Via XX Settembre and Via Tiraboschi.

Worth a look for **fashion** are Barbara Boutique (Via Broseta (52), Berne (Via Borfuro 6), Cinquini Moda (Viale Giovanni XXIII 88) and Tizian Fausti in Il Sentierone. Cinquini Moda is also good for lingerie. For **leather goods** try Gianfranco Pelle (Via XX Settembre 120) and the Tiziana Fausti shop at Piazza Della Libertà 10. The latter is good for exclusive shoe styles. For **jewellery** try Annavi (Via Sant'Orsola 12) and Bossio Gioelleria (Galleria Santa Marta 3, B 035 244324).

Brescia

The shopping in Brescia is centred around Corso Zanardelli at the heart of the old town.

Good local **fashion** shops include Alexander (Via Gramsci 19), Lanificio Luigi Colombo (Corso Magenta 32A), Massardi (Via Mazzini 32) and Valeria Boutique (Corso Zanardelli 16). For **leather** try Caruso (Piazza Mercato 16A) or Folli Follie (Via Cavalotti 1), or for shoes Apollo (Via Appollonio 5) and Castagna (Corso Cavour 7C). Finally, for **jewellery** Barozzi (Corso Garibaldi 26 and Via Gramsci 16) and Veschetti

(Corso Magenta 27E) are worth considering.

Verona

The main shopping area is Via Mazzini – which links Piazza Brà to Via Cappello, and, close by, Piazza Erbe and Piazza dei Signori.

For **fashion** items the best shops are Al Duca D'Aosta (Via Mazzini 31), Alexandra (Vicolo Mazzini 4 and 11), Belfe & Belfe (Via Pellicciai 28), Carla (Via Quattro Spade 7), Class Uomo (Via San Rocchetto 13B – menswear), L'Angolo 11 (Via Pelliciai 11) and Novella (Via Carlo Cattaneo 18). For **leather**, try La Piazzetta (Piazzetta Peschiera 10) and Valextra (Piazza Delle Erbe 23) or, for shoes, Ballin (Via Mazzini 33). Tapparini (Corso Porta Borsari 12) and Gioielli Soprana (Via Rosa 4B) are worth considering if you are looking for **jewellery**.

The Lakes

Some of the most interesting places for visitors to shop in the lakes area are 'factory shops', where famous brand names sell their wares at factory prices. The most famous of these shops are:

Armani, the fashion house
Fino Mornasco exit from the A9 autostrada (from A8 to Como)

Colombo, the cashmere house
Romagnano Sesia exit of the A26 autostrada (Alessandria to Gravellona Toce)

Ratti, the silk makers
Lomazzo exit of the A9 autostrada (from A8 to Como)

Rosetti, the shoe makers
At Parabiago – Legnano or Castellanza exits of the A8 autostrada (Varese to Milan)

Sergio Tacchini, the sportswear company

At Gravellona Toce, near Lake Maggiore

Como is the best place for **silk** – try Frey (Via Boldoni 36 and Via Garibaldi 10), Mantero (Via Volta 68) or Picci (Via Vittorio Emanuele 54).

For something different:

Lake Maggiore
Studio Sergio Tapia Radic
✉ **18 Brezzo di Bedero**
☎ **0332 508284**
This Chilean-born sculptor is enjoying growing acclaim throughout Europe. Call for an appointment.

Candele d'Arte
✉ **Via Del Porto 12, Luino**
☎ **0332 530784**
Here you can watch beautiful candles being made.

Luino also has a leather market every Wednesday.

Lake Como
Arte e Moda
✉ **Salita Mella 19, Bellagio**
☎ **031 950067**
Here Pierangelo Masciadri sells scarves and ties with original patterns based on ancient and Renaissance works.

Arte Orafa
✉ **Salita Mella 23, Bellagio**
☎ **031 951177**
Giuseppe Stelitano makes highly original jewellery.

Lake Garda
Lo Scrigno
✉ **Piazza Flaminia 14**
☎ **030 916243**
The place for beautiful jewellery, some in pure silver (rather than the more usual silver-nickel mix).

Wine & Olive Oil
There will be an *enoteca* (wine shop) in any village of reasonable size. There is also likely to be an *alimentari*, where you can buy olive oil.

Siestas
Italy's Mediterranean climate – and despite the closeness of the Alps, it can be very warm on the Lakes in summer – means that the idea of a siesta flourishes. Shops close for two, sometimes three, hours around midday allowing the staff to relax during the hottest part of the day. This can come as a surprise to visitors from the cooler north of Europe, but there is a compensation: during the evening the shops stay open late, until at least 7PM, sometimes even later.

Children's Attractions

Carnivals

The carnival season will delight most children who are in the lakes area during March. All the carnivals have floats, but for the local children the greatest entertainment is found in covering each other with foam from spray cans. The foam is harmless – though it creates a lot of washing. After a typical carnival the foam will be ankle deep on the pavement and every child in sight will be a walking foam ball, topped off with liberal amounts of confetti.

Children are not well catered for around the western lakes, particularly Lake Como where specific attractions are non-existent. However, although not aimed specifically at children, all the lakes offer the chance to learn how to windsurf, waterski or undertake other water sports and there are cable cars to the high ridges where exciting walks are usually possible.

Lake Maggiore and Lake Lugano

Villa Pallavicino

The park has a zoo with 40 species of animal, most of which are free to roam. Children can get close to the more docile animals, or make the most of the well-equipped playground.

✉ **Via Sempione 61, Stresa**
☎ **0323 32407/31533** 🕐 **Daily 9–6**

Zoo Safari del Lago Maggiore

A conventional safari park with lions, tigers, giraffes, white rhinos, camels and much more. There is also an aquarium with fish from Lake Maggiore and, in case it all seems a bit tame, piranhas.

✉ **Just off SS (Stradale Statale) 32 (Arona-Novara) at Pombia, about 15 minutes drive from Arona** ☎ **0321 956431**
🕐 **Daily 10–7 (11–4 winter)**

Funivia to the Mottarone

The cable car offers a great ride, and a great view, though unfortunately there is limited potential for walking at the top.

✉ **Piazza Stazione 1, Stresa**
☎ **0323 30399** 🕐 **Daily 9–5:30**

Doll Museum

A charming museum for children keen on dolls.

✉ **Angera Castle, Via alla Rocca, Angera** ☎ **0332 931300**
🕐 **Mar–Nov 9:30–5:30 (5 in Oct and Nov)**

Museo dell'Ombrello e del Parasole

This unusual little museum might also enthral children. Gignese, a village above Stresa, was once the world's leading centre for the making of umbrellas and parasols, and the museum is devoted to the history of their design and use in fashion.

✉ **Piazza Museuo dell'Ombrello, Gignese**
☎ **0323 59209** 🕐 **Apr–Sep daily 10–12, 3:30–6:30**

Swissminiatur

The site will delight children of all ages with its display of the main sites of Switzerland at a scale of 1:25. The site is threaded by over 3km of model railway.

☎ **091 6401060** 🕐 **Mid-Mar to Oct, daily 9–6**

Museo del Cioccolato (Chocolate Museum)

A good standby in the event of rain. Watch the manufacture of chocolate and taste the end product.

✉ **Caslano** ☎ **091 6118856**
🕐 **Daily 9–6 (5, Sat and Sun)**

Lake Como

Apart from the railway from Como to Brunate and the cable car from Argegno to Pigra there is very little for children. The grounds of Villa Olmo are good for running off surplus energy, while the mountains of the Grigna and Resegone offer really exciting walks.

Lake Garda

Gardaland

Celebrating its 25th anniversary in 2000, Gardaland has everything, with gigantic roller coasters and numerous water rides topping the bill. Space Vertigo involves a 40m free fall drop guaranteed to test the strongest stomach. There are shows (including dolphins), bands, rides and much more. Day, multi-day and evening tickets available. These are not cheap, but once inside everything except food and drink is free.

✉ **Castelnuovo del Garda, near Peschiera del Garda** ☎ **045 6449777** ⏰ **Late Mar–Oct daily 9:30–6:30 (open until midnight, late Jun, all of Jul and early Aug). Also open Sat and Sun in Oct 9:30–7**

Caneva World

Calling itself 'Aqua Paradise' because it is largely water-based, with slides, pools and rides. Fun for adults as well.

✉ **Via Fassalta 1, Lasize (very close to Gardaland)** ☎ **045 7590633** ⏰ **May–Sep daily 9:30–7**

Parco Acquatico Cavour

Another aqua park with pools and a 'turbo' slide, great for cooling off in the summer months. Good facilities for both older and younger children as well as fast food and restaurants.

✉ **Borghetto, near Valeggio Sul Mincio, which lies 10km south of Peschiera del Garda** ☎ **045 7951880** ⏰ **Mon–Sat 9–12:30, 3–6:30 (closed pm Mon and Sat)**

Acquapark Altomincio

Superb park with an array of water slides, some awesomely long and breathtakingly fast. Good facilities for younger children and excellent pizzeria/restaurant

✉ **Via del Pilandro, San Martino della Battaglia** ☎ **045 7945131** ⏰ **Late May–early Sep daily 10–7**

Parco Acquatico Le Ninfee

Another fine set of slides and pools. Good facilities for younger children and excellent food outlets.

✉ **Near Desenzano del Garda** ☎ **030 9910414** ⏰ **May–mid-Sep daily 10–7**

Benacus, Il Monde dei Giochi

At night this is a disco and bar, but during the afternoon it is a good place for younger children, with slides, climbing frames etc and go-karts for older children. There is also a full set of video games.

✉ **Near Pastrengo, to the east of Lasize** ☎ **045 6770274** ⏰ **Tue–Sun 10–2am**

South Garda Karting

The best of Garda go-karting. Good restaurant on site.

✉ **At Lonato, on the SS567 about 5km south of Desenzano del Garda** ☎ **030 3753420/ 293027** ⏰ **Mid-Apr to mid-Oct daily 12–7, then for private hire during the evening until midnight**

Parco Natura Viva

A safari park with a fine collection of animals, including a pets' corner. There are also full-sized models of dinosaurs.

✉ **Loc. Figaro, 40, Bussolengo, near Pastrengo, to the east of Lazise** ☎ **045 7170113**

Public Toilets

Public toilets are in very short supply in all but the largest towns. To get over this, which causes an inevitable problem for children, the best idea is to ask at a café. Most of the smaller bars will not have toilets, but most cafés and all restaurants will. Buying a coffee usually smoothes the path.

Sport & Leisure

Pickpockets

It pays to be cautious in Italy's big cities, especially Milan. Pickpockets roam the pedestrianised streets of Milan's shopping quarter and the narrow streets of other towns where visitors congregate. That said, the visitor is at no more risk than in any other European city and the usual precautions – don't leave purses on display on top of bags and be careful about where you put your wallet – should ensure a trouble-free visit.

Watersports

'Sport' in the lakes area tends to mean watersports, particularly diving, windsurfing, sailing and waterskiing. The winds are dependable, blowing from the north in the mornings and from the south in the afternoons and evenings. In general, the further north on the lake you are the more dependable the weather. Add the sun and warmth and the area is almost ideal for watersports. The only drawback is that the lakes are fed by glacial and snow melt and so the water tends to be cold below the surface layer. Swimmers will usually find the water pleasantly warm, but divers or those falling off a surfboard are likely to disagree. The water is not super clear, but does have the advantage of having no tides, which makes it good for those learning to dive. As with all such areas, schools offering tuition in watersports tend to spring up and disappear with the season. Local tourist offices will be able to help with addresses in your area.

Diving

Asso Sub Il Pellicano
✉ Via Mazzini 43, Desenzano del Garda ☎ 030 9144449

Centro Subacqueo Abysso International
✉ Via 42 Martini 886, Verbania ☎ 0323 586240

Mutevole
✉ Via Partigiani 4, Mandello ☎ 0341 700769

Sporting Club Porto Moniga
✉ Moniga del Garda ☎ 0365 502364

Squadra Nautica di Salvamento
✉ Piazzale Flai 1, Verbania ☎ 0323 519100

Sailing

Circolo Vela Torbole
✉ Via Lungolago Verona 6, Torbole ☎ 0464 505350

Club Nautico Stresa
✉ Via Semipone Sud 17, Stresa ☎ 0323 30551

Nautica Spluga
✉ Valmadrera, to the west of Lecco ☎ 0341 201313

Scuola Nautica Voltiana
✉ Via Garibaldi 15, Como ☎ 031 273344

Windsurfing

Nautic Club Riva
✉ Viale Rovereto 44, Riva del Garda ☎ 0464 552453

Surf Centre
✉ Lido di Arco, Torbole ☎ 0464 505963

Surf Centre Lido Blu
✉ Via Foci del Sarca, Torbole ☎ 0464 505180

Surfin Progress
✉ Via Case Sparse 54, Domaso ☎ 0344 96208

Tomaso Sail and Surf
✉ Casali Darbedo 10, Cannobio ☎ 0323 72214

Windsurfercenter Domaso
✉ Via Case Sparse ☎ 0380 7000010

Waterskiing

Centro Sci Nautico Como
✉ Waterfront, Cernobbio ☎ 0335 6829850 or 031 342232

Club Nautico Stresa
✉ Via Semipone Sud 17, Stresa ☎ 0323 30551

Activities on Land

Canyoning

The gorges to the north of Lake Garda are ideal for the exacting sport of canyoning. This potentially dangerous sport should not be attempted alone by beginners. Visitors should be very cautious when selecting a group or leader for a trip. Ask for advice at the local tourist office.

Climbing

The Grigna peaks and the mountains north of Riva del Garda, around Arco, are famous for their rock-climbing. There are clubs, but limited facilities for those wanting to learn to climb. One of the most impressive facilities for beginners and experts alike is at Macagno, at the northern end of Lake Maggiore's eastern shore. Here a selection of cliffs and a bridge have been augmented with indoor climbing holds and protected by in situ bolts to create a remarkable climbing area. Tuition is available here, either by the hour or the day ☎ 0339 4373186 or 0335 6962338.

A Via Ferrata is, literally, an iron road, a section of cliff which has been rigged with ladders and pegs to allow mere mortals (most definitely only those with a head for heights, however) to explore places they would otherwise have no hope of reaching. Vie Ferrate are fully protected by wires running beside the ladders or across sections where climbers can more easily ascend. To make full use of a Via Ferrata, it is necessary to have a kit that allows the climber to be continuously clipped into the safety line, and to absorb the impact in the event of a fall. This kit requires a full climbing harness to be worn.

Although the heartland of Vie Ferrate is further northeast in the Dolomites, there are excellent routes on the Resegone and Monte Grona, both above Lake Como, and in the Brenta Dolomites to the north of Lake Garda.

Golf

Golf is increasing in popularity in Italy, and, with the climate and the magnificent views from some of the local courses, the visitor with an enthusiasm for the game is well catered for. Tourist offices will have a list of local clubs, but some popular ones are listed below.

Alpino di Stresa
🖂 **Vezzo, above Stresa**
☎ **0323 20642**

Arzaga
Only nine holes.
🖂 **Nr Padenghe sul Garda**
☎ **030 9913947**

Carimate
🖂 **At Lomazzo exit of the A9, south of Como** ☎ **031 790226**

Castelconturbia
🖂 **Agrate Conturbia, south of Arona** ☎ **0322 832093**

Dei Laghi
🖂 **Travedonna Monate, near Lake Monate, west of Varese**
☎ **0332 978101**

Desenzano del Garda
🖂 **Solano del Lago** ☎ **0365 674707**

Des Iles Borromées
✉ Brovello Carpugnino, above Stresa ☎ 0323 929285

Franciacorta
✉ Toscalano Maderno
☎ 030 984167

La Pinetina
✉ Appiano Gentile, south of Como ☎ 031 933202

La Robinie
✉ Solbiate Olona, south of Varese ☎ 0331 329260

Lecco
✉ Annone Brianza ☎ 0341 579525

Menaggio & Cadenabbia
✉ Menaggio ☎ 0344 32103

Monticello
✉ Cassina Rizzardi, southeast of Como ☎ 031 928055

Parco dei Colli
✉ Bergamo ☎ 035 250033

Piandisole
✉ Premeno, near Cannero Riviera ☎ 0323 587100

Varese
✉ Luvinate, to the west of the city ☎ 0332 229302

Villa d'Este
✉ Montorfano, southeast of Como ☎ 031 200200

Horse Riding

Horse riding on the ridges above the lakes is popular. The local tourist office will be able to provide details of stables.

Mountain Biking

Piedmont, Lombardy and Trentino have all produced booklets of suggested itineraries for mountain bikers, and bikes and guides can be easily hired. The majority of these are at the northern end of Lake Garda, which is a popular destination for adventure enthusiasts.

Parapenting/ Paragliding

The dependable winds which help the windsurfer and sailor also help the flyer. The high ridges also help deploy the flyer's parachute making the lakes a great area for beginners.

Brixia Flying
✉ Via San Zeno 117, 25124 Brescia ☎ 030 2420912

Skiing

There are numerous possibilities in winter – the 'real' Alps to the west of Lake Maggiore, the pre-Alps closer to the lake; the Grigna and Resegone peaks above Lake Como and the real Alps north of the lake; the high peaks which form the back walls of the Bergamo valleys; the ridges of Lake Garda, especially Monte Baldo. There are several ski schools near the lakes.

Walking

The ridges that define the lake valleys are excellent for walking, with several long-distance trails – for instance a four-day walk along the western ridge of Lake Como – and day walks. The harshest terrain is in the Val Grande near Lake Maggiore, on the Grigna peaks above Lake Como and on Monte Baldo which dominates Lake Garda's eastern shore. Easier walking is on the lower, more rounded ridges.

Nightlife

Casinos

Casino Municipale
✉ Via Villa 16, San Pellegrino Terme ☎ 0345 21404

Casino di Campione
✉ Campione d'Italia ☎ 091 6401111/6401118

Cinemas

There are cinemas in all the main cities and towns. Italian cinemas rarely show English language films with subtitles, usually dubbing an Italian sound track.

Discos

There are discos in most of the large towns on the lakes. As is the case everywhere, the most popular places change with the season if not the weather.

Milan

Plastic
✉ Viale Umbria 120
☎ 02 733996

Rock Hollywood
✉ Corso Como 15
☎ 02 6598996

Shocking
✉ Via Bastioni di Porta Nuova 12 ☎ 02 6595407

Lake Orta

Kelly Green
✉ Via Lungolago Gramsci 33, Omegna ☎ 0323 862917

Lake Maggiore

Patrizia
✉ Via Longhirolo 11, Luino
☎ 0332 533056

Tam Tam
✉ Piazza Flaim 16B, Intra
☎ 0323 403210

Torchio
✉ Via Darbedo 5, Cannobio
☎ 0323 71277

Varese

Griffe Club
✉ Via Dandolo 12, Varese
☎ 0332 238578

Lake Como

Charlie Brown
✉ Via San Giacomo 52, Como
☎ 031 241233

Le Streghe
✉ Salita Plinio 10/12, Bellagio
☎ 031 951648

Liberty
✉ Via Quattro Novembre, Dongo ☎ 034 481291

Brescia

Paradiso
✉ Via Casotti 12 ☎ 030 2302210

Lake Iseo

Dady Club
✉ Via Vittorio Veneto 9, Iseo
☎ 030 981977

Lake Garda

Art Club
✉ Via Mantova 1A, Desenzano del Garda ☎ 030 9991004

Chic a Boom
✉ Via Europa, Cunettone, Saló
☎ 0365 521076

ICS
✉ Peschiera del Garda
☎ 045 7551580

Tiffany
✉ Giardini di Porta Orientale, Riva del Garda ☎ 0464 552512

Theatres

There are theatres in all the major towns of the region. Some – Milan's La Scala and Verona's Arena – are world famous, but others, such as the Donizetti Theatre in Bergamo are equally good. It is very rare for productions in any of the theatres to be in a language other than Italian.

What's On When

Festivals

Two interesting festivals which involve medieval costumes are the Polio del Baradello at Como and the Compagne di Ballori at Ponte Caffaro, Lake Ledro. The Polio largely comprises boat and horse races but concludes with a spectacular procession through the city. The procession is always on a Sunday and usually coincides with the Italian Grand Prix. The Compagna, held in August, is a traditional music and dance festival with musicians in ancient dress playing old instruments. The event is accompanied by a day-long carnival.

The dates change, so consult the local tourist office.

3–5 January

Canto della Stella, Tignale, Lake Garda, re-enacts the journey of the Magi with a night-time procession accompanied by choirs.

31 January

Boat Festival, Orta San Giulio, Lake Orta

February

Carnival season. The most famous carnivals is at Venice. Within the Lakes' area, the best is at Verona (the *Gnoccho Bacchanalia*)

March

Autumn fashion collections, Milan

Lent

'Hag's Trials', Gargagno and Gardone, Lake Garda. The effigy of an old woman is burnt, a sad memorial of medieval life, though the event is now much jollier.

Easter

Processions in the Swiss villages of Lake Lugano often held on both Maundy Thursday and Good Friday.

9–10 April

Pageant to commemorate the creation of the Lombard League, Bergamo

c24 June

On the Sunday after St John the Baptist's Day, a boats process to Isola Comacina, Lake Como, for an outdoor mass in the ruined church.

June–July

Shakespeare season, Verona

July

Folklore Festival, Val Cannobina, Lake Maggiore

Festival of traditional music and dance, Quarna Sopra, Lake Orta
Jazz Festival, Lugano (first week in the month)
Music Festival, Lugano (last week in the month)
International Sailing Regatta, Gargagno, Lake Garda
Il Redentore: procession of gondolas and other craft at Venice, held over a weekend

July–August

Opera season, Verona, staged open-air in the Roman Arena.
Season of open-air plays at Il Vittoriale, Gardone Riviera, Lake Garda

Mid-August to mid-Sep

International Music Festival (Settimane Musicali), Stresa, Lake Maggiore. World famous event with top musicians and conductors

September to mid-Oct

Music Festival, Ascona, Lake Maggiore, timed so that some of the players from Stresa can appear again.

mid-September to Oct

Lake Maggiore villages celebrate a festival of local foods with special menus in the restaurants.

September

Grape Festival, Bardolino, Lake Garda (last weekend of month)
Firework Spectacular, Sirmione, Lake Garda

October

Spring fashion collections, Milan

7 December

First night of the opera season, Milan

Practical Matters

Above: *The car ferry on Lake Garda*
Right: *Tourist policeman, La Scala, Milan*

TIME DIFFERENCES

GMT 12 noon	Italy 1PM →	Germany 1PM →	USA (NY) 7AM ←	Netherlands 1PM →	Spain 1PM →

BEFORE YOU GO

WHAT YOU NEED

● Required
○ Suggested
▲ Not required

Some countries require a passport to remain valid for a minimum period (usually at least six months) beyond the date of entry – contact their consulate or embassy or your travel agency for details.

	UK	Germany	USA	Netherlands	Spain
Passport	●	●	▲	▲	▲
Visa (regulations can change – check before booking your journey)	▲	▲	▲	▲	▲
Onward or return ticket	▲	▲	▲	▲	▲
Health inoculations	▲	▲	▲	▲	▲
Health documentation (➤ 123, Health)	●	●	●	●	●
Travel insurance	○	○	○	○	○
Driving licence (national)	●	●	●	●	●
Car insurance certificate (if own car)	●	●	●	●	●
Car registration document (if own car)	●	●	●	●	●

WHEN TO GO

Como

High season

Low season

6°C	7°C	10°C	13°C	18°C	21°C	24°C	23°C	18°C	12°C	10°C	8°C
JAN	FEB	MAR	APR	MAY	JUN	JUL	AUG	SEP	OCT	NOV	DEC

🌧️ Wet ☁️ Cloud ☀️ Sun 🌦️ Sunshine/Showers

TOURIST OFFICES

In the UK
Italian State Tourist Board (ENIT) Offices
1 Princes Street
London, W1R 8AY
☎ 020 7408 1254
Fax: 020 7493 6695

In the USA
USA Suite 1565,
Rockefeller Centre,
630 Fifth Avenue
New York, NY 1011
☎ 212 245 4822
Fax: 212 586 9249

Suite 550,
12400 Wilshire Boulevard
Los Angeles
CA90025
☎ 310 820 1959
Fax: 310 820 6357

WHEN YOU ARE THERE

ARRIVING

At the time of writing the Italians are attempting to change the local international airport from Linate, to the east of Milan, to Malpensa, near the southern tip of Lake Maggiore. This move is being resisted by international carriers, as business passengers usually go to Milan. At present, therefore, most international carriers fly to both Linate and Malpensa, with fewer flights to the former. Each airport has bus connections to Milan from where the lakes can be reached by train. Linate is about 20 minutes from Milan, Malpensa is about an hour by bus and about 35 minutes by train. Train and bus times to the major lakes resorts from Milan are:

Como	Train 1 hour	Bus 1½ hours
Stresa	Train 1 hour	Bus 1½ hours
Desenzano	Train 1 hour	Bus 1 hour

Linate airport is 5km from Milan city centre. Note that If you are approaching Linate from the north, the slip road is on the left; that is, you exit from the outside (fast) lane. Malpensa airport is 55km from Milan city centre. The airport lies to the east of Gallarate, about 14km from the 'Busto Arsizio' exit of the A8 autostrada. For both airports ☎ 02 74852200

MONEY

The euro (€) is the official currency of Italy. Euro banknotes and coins were introduced in January 2002. Notes are issued in denominations of 5, 10, 20, 50, 100, 200 and 500 euros; coins in denominations of 1, 2, 5, 10, 20 and 50 cents, and 1 and 2 euros. Traveller's cheques are accepted by most hotels, shops and restaurants in lieu of cash, but the rate of exchange may be less favourable than in banks, which can be found in all towns and most villages.

TIME

 Italy is one hour ahead of Greenwich Mean Time (GMT+1), but from late March to late September daylight saving time (GMT+2) operates.

CUSTOMS

 YES
From another EU country for personal use (guidelines):
800 cigarettes, 200 cigars, 1 kilogram of tobacco
10 litres of spirits (over 22%)
20 litres of aperitifs
90 litres of wine, of which 60 litres can be sparkling wine
110 litres of beer

From a non-EU country for your personal use, the allowances are:
200 cigarettes OR
50 cigars OR 250 grams of tobacco
1 litre of spirits (over 22%)
2 litres of intermediary products (e.g. sherry) and sparkling wine
2 litres of still wine
50 grams of perfume
0.25 litres of eau de toilette
The value limit for goods is 175 euros.

Travellers under 17 years of age are not entitled to the tobacco and alcohol allowances.

 NO

Drugs, firearms, ammunition, offensive weapons, obscene material

UK
(02) 723001

Germany
(02) 6231101

USA
(02) 290351

Netherlands
(02) 4855841

WHEN YOU ARE THERE

TOURIST OFFICES

The main Tourist Offices are

Lake Maggiore
- Piazza Marconi 16
  28838 Stresa
  ☎ 0323 30150
  Fax: 0323 32561

- Via Piero Chiara 1
  21016 Luino
  ☎ 0332 530019
  Luino

Lake Como
- Piazza Cavour 17
  22100 Como
  ☎ 031 269712
  Fax: 031 240111

Lake Garda
- Corso Repubblica 8
  25083 Gardone Riviera
  ☎ 0365 20347
  Fax: 0365 20347

Riviera degli Olivi
- Via Don Gnocchi 23-25
  37016 Garda
  ☎ 045 6270384
  Fax: 045 7256720

- Giardini di P Orientale 8
  38066 Riva del Garda
  ☎ 0464 554444
  Fax: 0464 520308

- Corso Zanardelli 34
  25100 Brescia
  ☎ 030 43418
  Fax: 030 293284

Milan
- Via Marconi 1
  20123 Milano
  ☎ 02 725241
  Fax: 02 72524350

NATIONAL HOLIDAYS

J	F	M	A	M	J	J	A	S	O	N	D
2			2	1			1			1	2

1 January	New Year's Day,
6 January	Epiphany
Mar/Apr	Easter Sunday and Monday,
25 April	Liberation Day
1 May	Labour Day
2 June	National Day
15 August	Assumption Day
1 November	All Saints' Day
8 December	Immaculate Conception
25 and 26 December	Christmas

OPENING HOURS

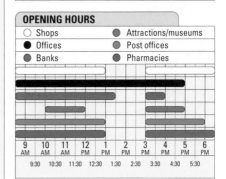

○ Shops   ● Attractions/museums
● Offices   ● Post offices
● Banks   ● Pharmacies

9 AM	10 AM	11 AM	12 PM	1 PM	2 PM	3 PM	4 PM	5 PM	6 PM
9:30	10:30	11:30	12:30	1:30	2:30	3:30	4:30	5:30	

Shops (including pharmacies) sometimes open later in summer. All shops usually close Monday morning. Post offices are usually open Saturday morning. Museums are usually open Sunday morning.

In addition to the above, large department stores, as well as supermarkets and shops in tourist areas, may open outside these times, especially in summer.

**DRIVE ON THE
RIGHT**

**TOILETS
FEW**

PUBLIC TRANSPORT

Flights
Italy has an excellent domestic air service operated by Alitalia. Book ahead as planes are crowded at the height of the summer season. Full-time students under 26 receive a 25 per cent discount on internal flight fares. For airport information at Malpensa or Linate ☎ 02 74852200. In addition to Malpensa and Linate airports, there are airports at Bergamo (Orta sul Serio) and Verona (Villafranca).

Trains
Italy has a good rail system. A 'Travel at Will' pass is available for 8, 15, 21 or 30 days. These offer unlimited travel on any train. Reduced rate passes are also available for visitors under 26 and senior citizens. Italy has various classes of train:
Super-Rapido/TEE Luxury First class only, running between major cities. Supplement charged. Seats must be pre-booked. **Rapido** Fast trains between major cities. Supplement charged. Seats may be pre-booked. **Espresso** Long-distance express trains. Limited stops. **Diretto** Slower, stopping at most stations. **Locale** Local, stopping at all stations. In addition to the main system, there are also a few private lines. Two of these link Como and Laveno to Milan.

Buses
The country also has a reasonable bus service. Passengers on city buses must buy a ticket before travelling – from bars or machines – and validate them on the bus by inserting them into a machine which overprints the date and time. The ticket allows unlimited travel for a set period. This is usually one hour.

Ferries
All the lakes have steamer services. Boat passes are available for 1 day, several days, 1 or 2 weeks. There are two types of boat. Hydrofoils (*aliscafo*) are fast, but do not stop at all villages. The slower boats stop more often, but even then not all the smaller villages are served by every boat.

CAR RENTAL

All the major car-hire companies are represented at Italian airports and railway stations and in the major towns and cities.

TAXIS

Taxis are available at all airports, railway and bus stations and at certain places within large towns and cities.

DRIVING

Speed limits on motorways:130kph (110kph for cars with engines below 1000cc)

Speed limit on main roads: 110kph; on minor roads: 90kph

Speed limit in urban areas: 50kph

Seat belts are obligatory for drivers and all passengers over the age of 7. Children under 12 years must travel in rear seats and restrained with an appropriate harness.

Random breath-testing. Limit is 80 micrograms of alcohol in 100ml of breath.

Petrol stations keep shop hours (though they may be open later in the evening). Even motorway petrol stations close at night. Very few petrol stations take credit cards except on the *autostradas*.

A red warning triangle must be carried and its use is obligatory in case of breakdown or accident. Police speedtrap detectors are illegal. Dipped headlights are compulsory in tunnels. To drive on Swiss motorways you most display a vignette, a tax disc valid for one year, available at border crossings and petrol stations.

The Touring Club of Italy (TCI), offer a breakdown service ☎ 116. If your car is hired, follow the hirer's instructions.

PERSONAL SAFETY

Italy has two police forces, the Polizia and the Carabinieri. The former is a standard police force, the latter a military-style force which deals with more serious crime. In practice, the visitor will be unable to distinguish between them. Visitors may also see Polizia Stradale, a specific highway force, and Vigili Urbani which operate within towns.

To help prevent crime:
- Do not carry more cash than you need.
- Do not leave valuables at the poolside
- Beware of pickpockets in tourist spots or crowded places
- Avoid walking alone at night in dark alleys of the large cities

Police assistance:
☎ 113 from any call box

ELECTRICITY

The power supply in Italy is 220 volts.

 Type of socket: round two-hole sockets taking round plugs of two round pins. British visitors will need an adaptor and US visitors will need a volatge transformer.

TELEPHONES

Public telephones take both coins and cards (though the latter are now much more common). Coin boxes usually take 200 and 500 lire coins.

International Dialling Codes

From Italy to:	
UK:	00 44
Germany:	00 49
USA:	00 1
Netherlands:	00 31

POST

Post offices are usually open Monday–Friday 8/8:30–1, 3–6 (Saturday 9–12)

TIPS/GRATUITIES

Yes ✓ No ✗		
Restaurants (10% usually included)	✓	10%
Cafes/Bars (if service not included)	✓	change
Tour Guides	✓	€2–3
Hairdressers	✓	change
Taxis (10% usually included)	✓	10%
Chambermaids	✓	€1
Porters	✓	€1–2
Theatre/Cinema Usherettes	✓	change
Cloakroom attendants	✓	change
Toilets	✓	change

PHOTOGRAPHY

What to photograph: buildings in the old town and village centres, lake scenes, lakes from mountains, mountain scenes.
Best time: all day. The lakes and mountains look good in both early morning light and at sunset. In high summer there is usually a heat haze and so early morning and early evening are to be preferred.
Where to buy film: films and batteries are readily available in tourist and photographic shops.

HEALTH

Insurance
Nationals of EU and certain other countries can get free medical treatment in Spain with the relevant documentation (Form E111 for Britons) although private medical insurance is still advised and is essential for all other visitors.

Dental Services
The E111 form covers dentistry as well. However, visitors with their own dental health insurance should obtain advice from their insurers.

Sun Advice
In northern Italy the summers can be hot and visitors should take all usual precautions against the sun – not going out in the middle of the day, wearing a hat and suncream, and drinking plenty of water.

Drugs
Medicines for personal use only are allowed through customs. Many prescription and non-prescription drugs are available from pharmacies.

Safe Water
Italian water is completely safe. However, because of the sterilisation processes, which can affect the taste, many people buy mineral water (*acqua minerale*), which is readily available.

CONCESSIONS

There are some special student and senior citizen concessions in Italy – travel, museums etc. It is worth inquiring about these at the local Tourist Office. See also Public Transport, p. 121.

CLOTHING SIZES

Italy	UK	Rest of Europe	USA	
46	36	46	36	Suits
48	38	48	38	
50	40	50	40	
52	42	52	42	
54	44	54	44	
56	46	56	46	
41	7	41	8	Shoes
42	7.5	42	8.5	
43	8.5	43	9.5	
44	9.5	44	10.5	
45	10.5	45	11.5	
46	11	46	12	
37	14.5	37	14.5	Shirts
38	15	38	15	
39/40	15.5	39/40	15.5	
41	16	41	16	
42	16.5	42	16.5	
43	17	43	17	
36	8	34	6	Dresses
38	10	36	8	
40	12	38	10	
42	14	40	12	
44	16	42	14	
46	18	44	16	
38	4.5	38	6	Shoes
38	5	38	6.5	
39	5.5	39	7	
39	6	39	7.5	
40	6.5	40	8	
41	7	41	8.5	

WHEN DEPARTING

- Remember to contact the airport on the day prior to leaving to ensure the flight details are unchanged.
- Italian customs officials are usually polite, but rarely willing to negotiate

LANGUAGE

The language you hear on the street will be Italian, even if you are on the Swiss shores of Lakes Maggiore and Lugano. There are dialects in the mountains, but even there Italian is the first language. In Italian each syllable is pronounced, so *colazione* would be *col-atz-i-own-ay*. *C* and *g* are always 'hard' (as in cat or gate) before *a*, *o* or *u*, and always 'soft' (as in cello or gin) before *e* or *i*. To get a hard *c* or *g* before an *e* or *i*, Italians insert an *h*, eg Chianti. *Gn* is pronounced *ny*, like the Spanish *ñ* or Portuguese *nh*, so, for example, Campagna is pronounced Campanya.

hotel	*albergo*	reservation	*prenotazione*
bed and breakfast	*camera e la colazione*	room service	*servizio nella stanza*
single room	*singola*	bath	*bagno*
double room	*matrimoniale*	shower	*doccia*
one night	*una notte*	toilet	*gabinetto*

bank	*banca*	traveller's cheque	*traveller's cheque*
exchange office	*cambio*	credit card	*carta di credito*
post office	*ufficio postale*	exchange rate	*corse del cambio*
coin	*moneta*	commission charge	*commissione*
banknote	*banconote*		
cheque	*cheque*		

café	*caffè*	starter	*antipasto*
bar	*bar*	main course	*piatto*
breakfast	*colazione*	dessert	*dessert*
lunch	*pranzo*	bill	*conto*
dinner	*cena*	beer	*birra*
table	*tavolo*	wine	*vino*
waiter	*cameriere*	water	*acqua*
waitress	*cameriera*	coffee	*caffè*

aeroplane	*aereo*	single ticket	*andante*
airport	*aeroporto*	return ticket	*andante e ritorno*
train	*treno*	non-smoking	*non fuma*
station	*stazione*	car	*machina*
bus	*autobus*	petrol	*benzina*
bus stop	*fermata d'autobus*	how do...? I get to...?	*come si va a.*
boat	*battello*	where is...?	*dove si trova...?*
ticket	*biglietto*		

yes	*si*	how are you ?	*come sta ?*
no	*non*	do you speak English?	*parla inglese ?*
please	*per favore*	I don't understand	*non capisco*
thank you	*grazie*		
welcome	*benvenuto*	how much ?	*quanto costa ?*
goodbye	*arrivederci*	open	*aperto*
good morning	*buongiorno*	closed	*chiuso*
good afternoon	*buongiorno*	today	*oggi*
goodnight	*buona sera*	tomorrow	*domani*
you're welcome	*prego*		

Acknowledgements
The Automobile Association wishes to thank the following photographers and libraries for their assistance in the preparation of this book.

MARY EVANS PICTURE LIBRARY 10b, 11b, 14b; **PICTURES** 93t; **ROCCA BORROMEO** 43;
RICHARD SALE 2, 6b, 8b, 9b, 12b, 13c, 13b, 17b, 19b, 20b, 21b, 24b, 25b, 26b, 27t, 27b, 29b,
32b, 33b, 34b, 35b, 40b, 41b, 42b, 45, 47b, 48b, 50b, 51b, 52, 53, 55b, 58b, 60b, 62b, 63b, 64b,
65, 66b, 67b, 69b, 70b, 71b, 76b, 77b, 81, 82b, 83b, 85b, 86, 87, 88b, 90b, 91; **SPECTRUM
COLOUR LIBRARY** 93b; www.euro.ecb.int/ 119 (euro notes).

The remaining photographs are held in the Association's own library (**AA PHOTO LIBRARY**)
and were taken by **PETE BENNETT** with the exception of the following: **STEVE DAY** 49;
CLIVE SAWYER 5b, 7b, 15b, 16b, 18b, 22b, 23, 28, 29t, 32t, 33t, 34t, 35t, 38, 60a, 75, 122bl,
BARRIE SMITH 122t; **TONY SOUTER** 9b, 78b, 79, 122br.

Page layout: Jo Tapper **Edition managing editors:** Apostrophe S Limited